THE EVERYTHING KIDS' BASEBALL BOOK

Star players, great teams,
baseball legends, and tips
on playing like a pro

Rich Mintzer

Adams Media Corporation
Holbrook, Massachusetts

Acknowledgments

When I was eight I went to my first baseball game at Shea Stadium. I have no idea whether the Mets won or lost, but coming out of the tunnel into the mezzanine and seeing the giant green field for the first time in person is something I'll never forget. I've been a tremendous fan of baseball for many years. I've followed the teams, kept up with the statistics, collected baseball cards in the '60s and '70s (and yes, I still have the cards), joined a fantasy league, and now enjoy watching the ballgames with my son, Eric. My dad loved baseball, my sister was a fan when we were kids, my wife grew up a Mets fan, and my kids enjoy the game today. It's truly a game that spans the generations. Baseball is a marvelous interest to share with friends and family.

I want to thank my dad for taking me out to the ballpark, my mom for saving my baseball cards all these years, and my wife for her patience while I wrote and edited this book, which is dedicated to Eric and Rebecca, who checked it out to make sure it was "kid tested."

An Everything® Series Book.
Everything® is a registered trademark of Adams Media Corporation.

Published by Adams Media Corporation
260 Center Street, Holbrook, MA 02343
www.adamsmedia.com

ISBN: 1-58062-489-8

Printed in the United States of America.

J I H G F E D C B A

Library of Congress Cataloging-in-Publication Data
Mintzer, Richard
Everything kids' baseball / Rich Mintzer
p.   cm.
1. Baseball—United States—Juvenile literature. [1. Baseball.] I. Title.
GV867.5 .M56 2001
796.357—dc21   00-049608

Cover illustrations by Joseph Sherman.
Interior illustrations by Kurt Dobler and Kathie Kelleher.
Puzzles by Beth Blair.
Series editor: Cheryl Kimball

Puzzle Power Software by Centron Software Technologies, Inc. was used to create puzzle grids.

This book is available at quantity discounts for bulk purchases.
For information, call 1-800-872-5627.

See the entire Everything® series at *everything.com*.

Table of Contents

Introduction

There is nothing quite like baseball. It is called the American Pastime, which means it is our country's favorite game. The game has been played for well over one hundred years and is popular with people of every age. Even people who know little about sports know names like Babe Ruth, Joe DiMaggio, and Mark McGwire. There are movies, stories, poems, songs, videos, and plenty of books about baseball. Fans can enjoy not only watching games, but reading about players, following their statistics, and collecting baseball souvenirs and baseball cards. From the little leagues to the major leagues, baseball is

more than just a game—it can be a big part of life to share and enjoy with friends and family. Sometimes it's fun to sit and share stories of the great game with your parents and grandparents. They can tell you about watching some of the great players in history like Willie Mays and Hank Aaron, and you can tell them about the big hit you got in little league. It is truly a game for all ages.

This book takes a look at the great game, including its history and the greatest stars of the past and present. There is information on scoring a game, the Hall of Fame, collecting baseball cards, and lots more! From the beginnings of baseball to the best baseball Web sites, you'll find plenty of information in The Everything® Kids' Baseball Book. You'll even be able to fill your parents in on stuff they don't know. Up front there is some basic info about playing the game. See what you can find to help you as a player or as a fan watching and understanding the game.

Inning 1
Playing the Game

WORDS to KNOW

Umpire: An umpire is the person who is refereeing the game or ruling on the plays in the game. The umpire rules whether a pitch is a strike or a ball, if a ball that is hit is fair or foul, or if a batter or runner is safe or out. It's a tough job, and many players and fans aren't too crazy about the poor umpires!

Some Basics

In some ways baseball is a very simple game. You try to hit the ball and run to first base or farther without getting called out. You try to move around the bases on hits by other players and score runs. Each team gets three outs per turn, or inning, and there are nine innings unless the score is tied and the game goes into extra innings. The team who gets the most runs wins, and runs come from getting hits and making it around all the bases without getting called out. There are nine players on each side.

There are several types of outs and several types of hits. The most common outs are:

Flyout: A fly ball caught in the air.

Line out: A line drive caught in the air.

Pop out: A ball that doesn't go very far out, but goes up high in the air and is then caught in the air.

Strikeout: Swinging and missing pitches or not swinging at pitches going over home plate that the umpire calls a strike a total of three times (three strikes and you're out).

Groundout: A ground ball hit to an infielder who throws the ball to first base before the batter touches the base.

There's much more to the basic rules of baseball, but you learn as you play and as you watch—that's what makes it so much fun.

Fun and Games

Batting Cage Game

When you go to a batting cage, you usually get 10 swings for a certain amount of money, sometimes more and sometimes less, depending on where you go. You and a friend can have a friendly game of batting cage baseball.

Here's how it works. Every time you make contact you get one point, even if you foul it off. Every time you hit it beyond the pitching machine it's two points. Every time you miss the ball, you lose one point.

The game helps you concentrate on making contact with the ball and not swinging for the fences every time you step up. As you make contact more and more, you'll be able to take bigger swings and get more two-pointers—you may also miss and lose some points. It's just for fun, so don't get frustrated.

Batter's Box: The batter's box is the chalk rectangular box on either side of home plate where the batter must stand when he or she is batting. There is one for left-handed batters and one for right-handed batters.

This is how your hands should look when you "choke up" on the bat.

Hitting

There are plenty of ways to stand at home plate (known as your batting "stance") and plenty of successful styles of hitting. Coaches will work with you to help you find the one that is best for you.

Often batters start off with what is called a "square" stance, which means you stand in the middle of the batter's box, feet comfortably apart and knees bent slightly. You can change as you feel more comfortable swinging the bat. If you watch professional ballplayers, you can see that they have many different stances.

Along with finding the right batting stance is finding the bat that is right for you. Heavier doesn't mean more power if it is slowing down your swing. Don't use a bat that is too heavy for you. On the other hand, a bat that is too light will let you swing too fast. Bats are usually between 26 and 34 inches long, and the best one is the one that's most comfortable for you to swing based on your height and weight.

Once you've got the right bat and the right stance, you'll hit best by keeping your weight on your back foot and stepping forward in the batter's box toward the pitcher, or "into the pitch," as you begin your swing.

As you step, you pivot your hips and your arms swing . . . the bat follows your hips. Then your wrist snaps the bat through as it makes contact with the ball.

It's important to keep your eye on the ball as you try to make contact. You need to determine, while the ball is coming to you from the pitcher, where it is going to cross the plate, or if it is not going to be a pitch you should swing at at all. You have less than a second to make that decision.

Try to swing levelly, meaning don't try to swing in such a way to hit the ball up or down. If you can develop a

level swing and meet the ball for solid line drives you'll be off to a good start. Follow through after meeting the ball (meaning continue your swing around after making contact with the ball) and you'll increase your power. A level swing hit hard can result in hitting the ball a long way, too, and you can get the ball up in the air for a home run if it's hit just below the center. You'll see.

Don't get discouraged!

If you're having a hard time meeting the ball, "choke up" or move your hands up on the bat to get better bat control. You do not have to worry about hitting for power until you get comfortable meeting the ball. Many good hitters will choke up and get a single when they have two strikes rather than taking a big power swing and risk striking out.

Hitting is an art. Practice and enjoy it. And *always* wear a batting helmet.

> **Advice from the Best**
>
> Ty Cobb was perhaps the best hitter ever. He recommended that hitters not hold the bat at the bottom. Move your hands an inch up, and also keep your hands an inch apart from each other for better balance and bat control. He hit .367 and made the Hall of Fame, so perhaps he gave good advice!

Base Running

A good base runner does three things well:

1. Pays close attention to what's going on on the field at all times
2. Pays attention to the first and third base coaches
3. Doesn't get caught off the base

Base running looks easier than it is. Besides stepping on every base on your way around, you need to remember a lot of things. For example:

WORDS to KNOW

Cleanup Hitter: The cleanup hitter is the fourth hitter in the lineup.

Pinch Hitter: A pinch hitter is a hitter who bats in place of someone else.

FUN FACT

Baseball Question and Answer

What does it mean when a hitter is in a slump?

A slump is when a hitter stops getting hits for a while. It happens to all hitters, even the best. Sometimes this can last for a few days and sometimes for a few weeks. Hitters will try all sorts of things to get out of a slump, from extra batting practice to good luck charms. They'll go with whatever works to get them to start hitting well again.

1. When you hit the ball you should always toss aside the bat (don't throw it) and run hard to first base, even if you think the ball is going to be caught.
2. If you're on a base and the ball is hit high in the air, don't run too far—if it's caught, you must get back to your base or you can be tagged out. After the ball is caught you can tag the base and move to the next one. This isn't easy, so let the coach tell you when to tag up and move to the next base.
3. If there's a runner on first base and a ground ball is hit, the runner must head to second base. If there is also a runner on second base, that runner also has to move toward third base. These runners are *forced*, meaning they must vacate the base where another runner is headed. If, however, you are on second base and no one is on first, when the batter hits the ball you aren't forced to move since no one is running to your base. Good baseball strategy says that if you are on second base and the ball is hit in front of you, meaning to shortstop or third base, you don't run since they can easily tag you out. But if the ball is hit behind you, to the second baseman or first baseman, you can take off for third base.
4. If there are two outs, forget all of the above and run on anything hit. Sometimes you'll be able to advance two bases, like from first to third or second to home plate, and score a run.

These are just the very basics. You also have to stay within the baselines, not interfere with a fielder making a play, and never pass a runner ahead of you or you'll be called out. Coaches will help you run the bases, so pay attention to their directions.

Run the Bases

Starting with number 1 and ending with 143, connect the dots to find the answer to the following riddle: Why do hitters like to play night baseball? Because there are more _____ to choose from!

7

Practice Pitching Ball

You can't use this ball in a game, but a company called Franklin sells a baseball with colored dots that show you exactly where to put your fingers to throw the different pitches. You might want ask your mom or dad if you can get a couple of these practice balls.

Base Stealing

Stealing bases is a whole art unto itself. It's when a base runner takes off and moves over to the next base while the pitcher is throwing the ball to the batter. The best base stealers know how to get a good lead, meaning they move a few steps away from the base and watch the pitcher carefully, since sometimes the pitcher turns and throws to your base to try to have the baseman tag you out while you're off the base. Good base stealers break for second or third base at the right moment—usually just as the ball is released toward home plate, they'll take off and slide into second or third base ahead of the throw from the catcher to the baseman. Practice sliding on soft dirt or sand with a coach showing you the proper way to slide. Don't just start sliding into bases without learning how to slide properly or you will get injured; even professional players who slide wrong get hurt.

WORDS to KNOW

Mound: The mound, or pitching mound, is the dirt circle in the middle of the infield diamond where the pitcher stands.

Count: The count is the number of balls and strikes that have been pitched to the hitter. For example, two balls and two strikes would be a "two and two" count.

Pitching

Like hitting, pitching is an art. It takes a lot of practice and concentration. The pitcher throws the ball to the batter until the batter either gets a hit or strikes out (misses three good pitches), or the pitcher throws four balls that are out of the strike zone, in which case the batter gets to walk to first base.

Naturally the idea is to get the batter out, but it's not so easy. You want to be able to throw pitches that the batter will swing at and miss. If you throw pitches wildly or out of the strike zone, you'll walk too many hitters and you won't be on the mound for very long. The strike zone is over home plate and generally from the batter's knees up to the chest area.

Fun and Games

Punchball

You use the same basic idea of baseball, but if you don't have gloves, bats, or a field handy, you can use a rubber ball or a tennis ball that bounces. Bounce it once, then swing your extended arm like a bat and punch the ball. Position as many fielders as you have at bases and in the outfield. You don't need a pitcher or a catcher, and if you don't have enough people to fill the other positions, you can shrink the field and only play with three bases and two outfielders (it's often hard to punch a ball into the outfield anyway). Punchball is a good alternative to baseball or softball if you're in a school yard looking for a baseball-like game to play with a bunch of friends.

Wiffle Ball Warm-Ups

Wiffle balls are plastic balls with holes in them that don't travel very far when you hit them. They make similar plastic balls for golf (generally without the holes). They are good to use when you don't have much room to practice, but you want to try hitting the ball. Have someone throw the wiffle ball to you underhanded and practice swinging at it—you won't hit it far, but it's a good chance to practice making contact and hitting the ball.

Different umpires will call different strike zones. The problem is that if the pitcher simply throws it right over home plate, there is a good chance the batter is going to smash it and get a hit. Charlie Brown in the Peanuts cartoon is famous for throwing his pitch right over home plate and having it hit back so hard that it knocks nearly all of his clothes off.

Since pitchers want to make their pitches hard to hit so that the batter will strike out or hit the ball to one of the fielders, they have developed several different types of pitches over the years, some of which are described below. Pitching takes a lot of practice, and new pitchers should learn under the guidance of a coach who knows the correct way to throw the pitch. Too many young pitchers hurt their arms every year trying to throw new pitches, trying to throw too hard, or trying to throw too many pitches in one day. Even major league pitchers are kept on a pitch count. That means someone in the dugout counts the pitches a pitcher is throwing and when the number gets too high for that pitcher he is taken out so he won't hurt his arm.

Pitchers also have to field ground balls hit to them and throw to first base for an out, or sometimes to another base for a forced out. It's also important for pitchers to keep an eye on the base runners so they don't go stealing too many bases. Here are some types of pitches:

- Fastball: A fastball is held with two fingers on the seams of the ball. Then you throw it hard and straight, making sure to follow through. The ball should roll off the tips of your fingers when released.
- Change-up: The other important pitch for young pitchers is the change-up. The ball is held with all the fingers a little further back in the hand, which will make the ball move

When You're Out, You're Out

Unlike basketball, hockey, or football where you can come out of a game for a rest and then return to the game, in baseball, when you are called out of the game you are out for the rest of that game.

more slowly. Mixing up a good fastball and a good change-up will confuse hitters because the pitches are at different speeds.

Once young pitchers get a little older, usually around 15 or 16 (it depends on the pitcher and proper coaching) you can learn a curve ball, slider, or screwball. A knuckleball is a special pitch thrown by only a few professional pitchers—the ball is held with the fingertips, and it floats to home plate. It moves around a lot and is hard to hit. It's also very hard to control as a pitcher.

The better major league pitchers have usually mastered two or three of these pitches and are able to throw the ball over any corner of home plate, so batters don't know where they will need to swing. They can also throw very hard, sometimes nearly 100 miles per hour. You should start off by working on your fastball and change-up until you throw mostly strikes and have mastered them both.

Defense

Each position has different responsibilities. Catchers not only catch the pitches, but also give the pitchers signals as to what pitch to throw next, block home plate and tag out runners trying to score, and (hopefully) throw out runners trying to steal. Catchers need to wear a special catcher's mitt, chest protector, shin guards, and a catcher's mask. The catcher is often the most important player defensively since he or she is involved in every play. A

FUN FACT

Important Reminder for Pitchers!

Remember, don't practice a curveball or other pitches besides the fastball and change-up until your coach feels you are ready. It's very easy to hurt your arm and ruin your chances at playing the game completely.

Little League Facts

Little League baseball began in 1939 in Williamsport, Pennsylvania, where the Little League World Series is still played today.

Little League baseball is popular with boys and girls ages 5 through 17. Nearly three million players around the world are on Little League teams. Teams usually have from 12 to 20 players, and everyone should get to play. Make sure you have fun and that the grownups don't take the game too seriously.

Fun and Games

Off the Wall

This is a fun game you can play with two people, a ball, a glove, and a wall. You don't even need a glove if you're using a softer ball like a tennis ball.

First you find a wall without windows or a "no ballplaying" sign. A vacant handball court may do or even the side of a barn if you don't live in the city. Next to the wall, you mark off a territory or use existing lines to designate what is fair and what is foul. Use an area that you can run from one end to the other in not too many steps.

To play, one player throws the ball high off the wall and the other person has to catch it. If the catcher catches the ball without it bouncing on the ground, he or she gets an "out." If the catcher drops it, the person throwing the ball has a runner on first base. If the ball bounces once before being caught, it's a single; twice, it's a double; three times, it's a triple; and four times, it's a home run. Always remember where your runners are, and keep track of how many runs you each score. Don't choose a space too big, or you'll never be able to cover the ground. Also, make a rule against throwing the ball so close to the wall that the only way to catch it is by crashing into the wall. Off the Wall is a fun game and a good way to practice covering ground in the outfield and catching fly balls.

catcher also has to be ready to field balls that are bunted—hit softly right in front of home plate—and foul balls that are popped up in the air behind home plate. It is definitely the toughest position, which might explain why there are always fewer people who want to be catchers.

Infielders need to work long and hard at fielding ground balls. If you can field the ball and throw the runner out at first base you're on your way to playing the infield. You'll also learn to turn a double play, especially if you're playing second base or shortstop. You'll have to take the throw from another fielder or get the ground ball and tag the base for one out, then throw to first base for the second out. If you're playing first base, you'll have to handle all kinds of throws from your fellow infielders. First basemen get bigger gloves, but sometimes even that doesn't help. If you're playing third base, you'll have to practice that long throw across the field to the first

WORDS to KNOW

Double play: A double play is when two players get called out after one player hits the ball.

Triple play: A triple play is a very rare play where one player hits the ball and all three outs are made. Naturally, there has to be no one out and at least two runners on base for a triple play.

Curve Ball

The curve ball is one of the trickiest pitches to hit. See if you can score by circling each of the curvy baseball terms in the following list! Instead of reading in a straight line, each word has *one* bend in it. Words can go in any direction. Hint: One word has been circled for you.

WORD LIST

ASTROTURF	POP FLY
BLEACHERS	SCOREBOARD
DUGOUT	SHORTSTOP
HOME RUN	STADIUM
HOT DOG	WORLD SERIES

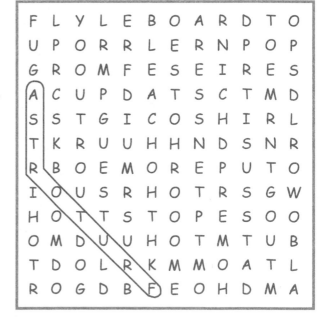

```
F  L  Y  L  E  B  O  A  R  D  T  O
U  P  O  R  R  L  E  R  N  P  O  P
G  R  O  M  F  E  S  E  I  R  E  S
A  C  U  P  D  A  T  S  C  T  M  D
S  S  T  G  I  C  O  S  H  I  R  L
T  K  R  U  U  H  H  N  D  S  N  R
R  B  O  E  M  O  R  E  P  U  T  O
I  O  U  S  R  H  O  T  R  S  G  W
H  O  T  T  S  T  O  P  E  S  O  O
O  M  D  U  U  H  O  T  M  T  U  B
T  D  O  L  R  K  M  M  O  A  T  L
R  O  G  D  B  F  E  O  H  D  M  A
```

Picture This #1

This combination of pictures "spells" a well known baseball place.

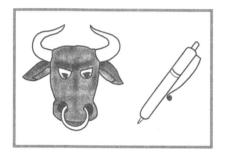

baseman. All infielders will also need to catch line drives and pop-ups. When the ball is in the air, call out "I got it" so the other fielders don't crash into you. Sometimes the catcher or pitcher will yell which fielder should make the catch.

Outfielders need to work on catching fly balls. A good outfielder picks up the direction of the ball just as it comes off the bat and is headed in their general direction. Learning how to judge where a fly ball is going is the first step, running over there and then making the catch follows. Outfielders also need to know how to play a ball that bounces in front of them or hits off the wall behind them. It's important to get to the ball quickly and turn and throw to the "cutoff player," which is one of the infielders who will catch your throw and then turn and throw to the base where the runner is headed. Each outfielder should know who his or her cutoff player is. Sometimes you'll see a runner trying to score and you'll want to make that long throw from the outfield to home plate. Coaches and managers don't like it when you don't throw to your cutoff player, so you'd better be very sure you can make a really long throw if you dare try it—or you may find yourself on the bench for the next game.

The most important thing for defensive players to learn is fielding balls hit in the air and on the ground and to be alert at all times. You'll also need to back up your fellow fielders. Good defense is as much a part of the game as good hitting or pitching. Major leaguers just make it look so easy that often defense doesn't get noticed. Don't be fooled, it's not that easy, so practice your defense hard.

Inning 2

The History of Baseball

There are 30 major league teams today, with many more minor league teams with players hoping to make it to the big leagues. There are thousands of college teams, high school teams, and little league teams all playing baseball. Where did it all begin? How did the major leagues get started?

The Earliest Games

No one is quite sure who actually invented baseball. Some people believe that in 1839, when Abner Doubleday began playing a game called "town ball" in Cooperstown, New York, that baseball was born. This early game was based on the games Cricket and Rounders, both played in England. Other people, however, give credit to Alexander Cartwright, who in the early 1840s developed a game played on a diamond-shaped field with rules that more closely resemble the game we know as baseball. The game was played with players who ran from base to base after hitting the ball. There were foul lines, and if batters swung and missed three times, they were called out. Either way, Doubleday and Cartwright are both in their own ways given credit for beginning the game we love today.

On June 19, 1846, at Elysian Fields in Hoboken, New Jersey, the first official baseball game took place. Two amateur teams from New York City, the Knickerbockers and the New York Nine played a four-inning game, won by the Nine 23 to 1. Pitchers threw underhanded, no one had gloves, the ball was softer than what we know as a baseball today, and the bases were only 42 paces from each other—but it was baseball. The idea was to hit the ball, get from base to base safely, and score runs before getting three outs in your team's turn at bat.

Picture This #2

This combination of pictures "spells" a type of pitcher.

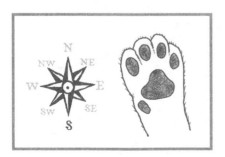

From that first game, baseball caught on quickly. Amateur teams were formed, and they played until the first team scored 21 runs, which at that time only took a few innings. In 1857 the idea of playing a nine-inning game was introduced, and more rules were changed. One of the most important changes was to put the bases 90 feet apart from each other. That is still the distance today. Somehow, for over one hundred years, it has always been exactly the right amount of feet to make it just hard enough to run to first base before the throw gets there from an infielder.

The 1850s was also the time when a writer named Henry Chadwick became the first baseball editor, writing about baseball, promoting the game, and inventing the box score that is still in newspapers (and on the Internet) today.

By the time the Civil War broke out, baseball was being played all over the country. Soldiers played the game during the war, making some changes to the rules. Around this time the idea of calling a ball for a bad pitch was introduced, and stealing a base also became part of the game.

As far back as 1870 there were barnstorming teams, which were teams that went from city to city playing each other. Then in 1871 the National Association of Professional Baseball Players was formed with nine teams. The Philadelphia Athletics were the first champions, winning 22 and losing only 7. By 1875 too much gambling caused people to lose interest in this league, but not in baseball. In 1876 the National League was formed. Many players from the original association became part of

Box Score: A box score is a grid containing a summary of the game statistics, including how each player did.

17

FUN FACT

The First Season

The first American League season was 1901. The National League had been around for more than 20 years. The winningest pitcher in that first official A.L. season was Cy Young, who won 33 games.

The Curse of the Bambino

Between 1903 and 1918, the Boston Red Sox won the World Series five times. Following the 1919 season, the Red Sox traded Babe Ruth ("the Bambino") to the New York Yankees. Since the trade the Red Sox have never again won the World Series. They've lost in the seventh game on four occasions but never won. They call this misfortune "the curse of the Bambino."

this new league, including "Cap" Anson, who was considered one of the game's first star players.

Through the 1880s and 1890s, several other leagues including the American Association, the Players League, and a minor league called the Western League began. All except for the Western League failed.

The National League, however, was a big success.

Baseball Through the Decades

1900–1909

In 1901 the Western League turned into the American League and started taking players from the National League. National League team owners were not too happy about this. The war between the two leagues lasted for two years, until they finally united in 1903 and created the concept of a World Series between the two leagues. The first series was played at the end of the 1903 season between the Pittsburgh Pirates of the National League and the Boston Pilgrims of the American League. The peace between the leagues didn't last long. The two leagues battled again over players and in 1904 cancelled the World Series. By 1905 they were reunited once again and have played the World Series ever since, with the exception of 1994 when the players went on strike.

The first decade of the 1900s featured a great Chicago Cubs team that in 1906 won 116 games and lost only 36. They played in three World Series

American League Domination

Nine All-Star games were played in the 1940s, and the American League won eight of them.

and won two of them. The Cubs featured an incredible infield combination that included Joe Tinkers, John Evers, and Frank Chance. They were so good at turning a double play that stories and poems were written about the famed combination of Tinkers to Evers to Chance. Meanwhile Nap Lajoie was the American League's first batting champion, with an incredible .422 batting average, topped only once ever since. The two biggest stars of the day were Ty Cobb in the American League and Honus Wagner in the National League. Both were great hitters and had tremendous speed, stealing plenty of bases. Top pitchers of the day included Cy Young, Christy Mathewson, and Ed Walsh. There were only five or six pitchers on a team, and starters pitched more often and for more innings than they do today. Hitters hit plenty of singles, doubles, and even triples, but home runs were not common, and league leaders had not topped 16 homers through 1910.

1910–1919

The second decade of the 1900s saw the world's attention drawn to the first World War. The major leagues had their own battle against a new league called the Federal League, which spent a couple of years taking players away from the American and National Leagues. Finally the major leagues were able to reach an agreement with this new league, and they were dissolved. The New York Giants were the top team in the National League, led by one of baseball's all-time great managers, John McGraw. In the American League the Philadelphia Athletics, led by their great manager Connie Mack, and the Boston Red Sox were the toughest teams.

Grover Alexander, Rube Marquade, and Walter Johnson became the top pitchers of the era. Johnson would go on to be one of the best, if not the best, pitcher ever. A young pitcher also

FUN FACT

Black Sox

In 1919 the Chicago White Sox became the Chicago Black Sox by allegedly throwing the World Series. Eight players on the White Sox were accused of being paid by gamblers to intentionally lose the series to the Reds. The case went to court, but a lack of solid evidence made it impossible for the court to send the guilty players to jail. The first commissioner of baseball, however, banned the eight players from the game forever. One of those players, "Shoeless" Joe Jackson, was one of baseball's all-time greatest hitters, but because he was kicked out of baseball, Jackson, who hit .356 through 13 seasons, is not in the Hall of Fame. The movie (available on video) *Eight Men Out* tells the whole story.

FUN FACT

Heinie Who?

In 1912, a relatively average ballplayer named Heinie Zimmerman of the Cubs got more hits, doubles, home runs, and RBIs and hit for a higher batting average than at any other time in his career. That one great year resulted in him becoming the Triple Crown winner, the only one since 1900 who isn't a Hall of Famer. It was one great year for Heinie.

Who Says Baseball Is a Slow Game?

In 1919 the New York Giants beat the Philadelphia Phillies 6 to 1 in only 51 minutes. That's amazing when you consider that most baseball games today take from two and a half to three hours.

appeared in 1917 and won 24 games to lead the league for the Boston Red Sox. They soon realized that this pitcher could hit, too. Two years later, as an outfielder, he would set a record with 29 home runs. The pitcher who became an outfielder was Babe Ruth. Until that time home run hitters were scarce, and no one hit more than 20 or 25. Ty Cobb, Tris Speaker, and Honus Wagner were the premier hitters in the pre-Babe era, but they were not hitting home runs like "The Babe."

1920–1929

After World War I, the country was in a time called the Roaring Twenties, filled with plenty of singing, dancing, and great baseball. The most popular player was "The Babe," who was a big hero everywhere he went and the first player to make as much as $50,000, which in those days was a very high salary.

The first three World Series played between the two New York teams were played in 1921, 1922, and 1923, and were called the Subway Series because fans could take the subway from one ballpark to the other. The Giants won the first two, but in 1923 the Yankees won their first of many World Series titles. For the next 41 years they would dominate baseball, winning 29 American League pennants during that time period. They won the World Series 20 of those 29 years. Miller Huggins was the manager of the incredible Yankees team of the '20s that saw one losing season in 1925 before becoming what many consider the greatest team ever, the '27 Yankees. The 1927 team won 110 games and lost just 44 with Lou Gehrig, Tony Lazzeri, Bob Meusel, and of course, Babe Ruth leading the offense, and Waite Hoyt leading the pitching staff. In 1927 Ruth hit 60 home runs, a record that would hold up for 37 years, and in 1929 Ruth became the first player ever to reach 500 home runs. Only 15 others have done it since.

The 1920s marked the beginning of home run hitters and the game became more exciting. Rogers Hornsby was the biggest star of the National League. Hornsby led the league six times in batting, winning the Triple Crown in 1922 (leading the league in home runs, RBIs, and batting average) and leading the Cardinals to their first trips to the World Series in 1926 and 1928. George Sisler, Hack Wilson, and Al Simmons were among the other top hitters of the decade, while Lefty Grove, Grover Alexander, and Dazzy Vance were among the best pitchers of their time.

Murderers' Row

There have been many great lineups in baseball history, but the greatest of them all is often considered to be the 1927 lineup of the New York Yankees, nicknamed "Murderers' Row." For those of you who like baseball statistics, look at the first big six in the lineup:

	HR	RBI	BA
CF Combs	6	64	.356
SS Koenig	3	62	.285
RF Ruth	60	164	.356
1B Gehrig	47	175	.373
LF Meusel	8	103	.337
2B Lazzeri	18	102	.309

And they had Waite Hoyt, a pitcher who won 22 games and posted a 2.63 ERA.

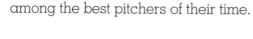

1930–1939

Times were difficult for many Americans in the 1930s because of the Great Depression. Many people were out of work and without much money. Baseball was still something to turn to for fun and to forget about the tough times. Al Simmons and Jimmie Foxx led a tough Philadelphia Athletics team with Foxx coming close to Ruth's home run record, hitting 58 homers in one season. The A's won the Series in 1929 and 1930 before losing to the Cardinals in 1931. In the National League, the Cubs' Hack Wilson would set a one-season record that still

FUN FACT

Uniform Numbers

The Yankees were the first team to wear numbers on their backs in the 1920s, and they were given those numbers by where they fell in the batting order. Babe Ruth always hit third, so he was number 3, and Lou Gehrig always hit fourth, so he was number 4, and so on. Today the number on a player's uniform has nothing to do with where the player bats in the order.

holds today, driving in 191 runs. The Giants, along with the Cubs, would find themselves losers to the Yankees, who won five more World Championships in the decade.

Babe Ruth would play his last game for the Yankees in 1934, then play a few with the Braves in 1935 before retiring. Ruth's teammate Lou Gehrig would continue to play alongside a new teammate who appeared in 1936, another baseball legend named Joe DiMaggio. Gehrig would retire because of a serious illness in 1937 after playing 2,130 consecutive games, a record that many thought would never be broken.

The 1930s was also a time when baseball began honoring the greatest players. The first ever all-star game was played on July 6, 1933, before 47,595 fans at Comisky Park in Chicago. Baseball also created the Hall of Fame in Cooperstown, New York, voting in five superplayers in 1936. The players, Ty Cobb, Babe Ruth, Honus Wagner, Christy Mathewson, and Walter Johnson were officially inducted in 1939 when the Hall of Fame officially opened.

One of the other most important changes to the game also took place in 1935 in Cincinnati when the first night game was played. The idea caught on fast and pretty soon many night games would appear on the schedule—except at Wrigley Field in Chicago where the owners, the Wrigley family, did not believe in night games.

1940–1949

World War II took over the world's attention during the 1940s, and many ballplayers would leave their teams to serve in the United States military. Young players and veterans who were too old for the military made up most of the teams. Since many of the men were in the army, women's baseball teams emerged, attracting a lot of attention as they played in their

own league. The movie *A League of Their Own* is based on this 1940s women's baseball league.

Before heading into the military, Ted Williams would establish himself as one of the greatest hitters ever, batting .406 in 1941. No one had batted .400 for 11 years, and no one has done it since. Williams, DiMaggio, and Bob Feller were baseball heroes and military heroes as well. Meanwhile, Stan Musial joined the Cardinals, who won four National League pennants and two World Championships in the '40s. The great rivalry between the Brooklyn Dodgers and the New York Yankees began as they met three times in the World Series, the Yankees winning all three.

But perhaps the most significant event in the decade for baseball was when, in 1946, Branch Rickey signed Jackie Robinson to a contract. Robinson was an African-American player, and until that time, no African-American player was allowed to play in the major leagues. Many great players, including Robinson, Cool Papa Bell, Josh Gibson, and Satchel Paige played in the Negro Leagues (see the section later in this chapter). There were many great players in these leagues, a number of whom would have been big stars in the major leagues if only the team owners would have let them play. Robinson would play for the minor league team, the Montreal Royals, in '46 and then join the major league's Brooklyn Dodgers team as the first ever African-American player in 1947.

1950–1959

World War II was over and singer Elvis Presley was known as "the King." Baseball was dominated by New York. Eight of ten World Series titles went to the New York teams, with the Yankees winning six times, the Giants once, and the Brooklyn Dodgers, after five tries, finally winning a World Series from the Yankees in 1955.

Rookie of the Year

Beginning in 1947 with Jackie Robinson, the best rookie (first year) player in each league was honored with the Rookie of the Year Award.

WORDS to KNOW

Pennant: The team that wins the National League or American League championship is said to have won the pennant—then they play in the World Series.

Triple Crown: When a player leads the league in home runs (HR), runs batted in (RBI), and batting average (BA) it's called winning the Triple Crown. It's only been done 16 times.

FUN FACT

The Shot Heard Around the World

The New York Giants and the Brooklyn Dodgers were tied for first place at the end of the 1951 season. They played one game to see which team would win the pennant and go to the World Series and which team would go home for the winter. The Dodgers led the game 4 to 1 going into the bottom of the ninth inning. The Giants got one run to make the score 4 to 2. Then up came Bobby Thompson against pitcher Ralph Branca, with two men on base. Thompson had hit 32 homers that season. Branca got strike one, and then it happened—Thompson connected, and the ball cleared the left field fence. Suddenly, just like that, the Giants had a 5 to 4 win and a trip to the World Series. This historic pennant-winning home run that became known as the Shot Heard Around the World.

Joe DiMaggio turned over the center field position on the Yankees to another future superstar, Mickey Mantle. Across the river from Yankee Stadium the New York Giants had a center fielder named Willie Mays, while in nearby Brooklyn the Dodgers had a guy named Duke Snider in center. Three Hall of Fame center fielders in one city! The Dodgers were loved by the people of Brooklyn. Along with Snider and Jackie Robinson, they had Roy Campanella as catcher, Gil Hodges at first base, Pee Wee Reese at shortstop, and Carl Furillo in right field. This was a terrific team that could do everything (except beat the Yankees).

The great New York baseball rivalries would come to a sudden end in 1957, when the Giants and the Dodgers both packed up their bags and headed out west to San Francisco and Los Angeles, leaving their devoted fans very sad. Air travel had become easier than traveling by train or bus, which teams had done for many years, so California got its first major league baseball teams. The Dodgers wasted little time and won the 1959 World Series. Another very important part of baseball in the 1950s was television. Until the 1940s people did not have television sets, but by the end of the decade they started becoming popular. In the 1950s more and more people owned television sets, and baseball was seen by millions of people.

Among the stars of the '50s were Henry Aaron, who would later go on to become the greatest home run hitter of all time in the 1970s, Al Rosen, Yogi Berra, Phil Rizzuto, Ernie Banks, Ed Mathews, Bob Lemon, Al Kaline, and Whitey Ford—plus Ted Williams and Stan Musial, who kept on going from the '40s.

1960–1969

The 1960s saw multicolored clothes and heard the great music of the Beatles. The 1961 Yankees were a powerhouse team, considered one of the greatest ever, winning 109 games

and losing only 53. Mickey Mantle was one of six players on the team to top 20 homers, with a tremendous 54. His teammate Roger Maris had even more, breaking Babe Ruth's record by hitting 61 homers. However, by 1965 the Yankees would finally start to fall, and by 1966 they were in last place.

The '60s was also a time for baseball growth, or "expansion," as it was called. More teams were added to the major leagues. The leagues each had eight teams for many years, and the season was 154 games long. In 1961 the American League added two new teams, one in Los Angeles called the Angels and the other in Washington called the Senators. There had been a Washington Senators team before, but they moved northwest to Minnesota. A year later, the National League added two new teams, the New York Mets and the Houston Colt 45s. New teams are usually not very good, but in 1962 the Mets, with manager Casey Stangel, who had managed many great winning Yankee teams, won only 40 games while losing 122 in the new 162-game season. It was the worst record ever, and the Mets were greeted with many appropriate jokes.

The Colt 45s, meanwhile, changed their name to the Astros and moved into a super new stadium called the Astrodome. It was the first indoor stadium, with fake grass called Astroturf and a modern scoreboard with all sorts of cool stuff going on. The Astrodome was, in the mid 1960s, something that seemed like it came from out of the future.

Some of baseball's greatest home run hitters played in the '60s, including Willie Mays, Willie McCovey, Hank Aaron, Ed Mathews, Frank Robinson, Ernie Banks, Mickey Mantle, and Reggie Jackson—all of whom topped 500 home runs. Roberto Clemente and Pete Rose would prove themselves as two incredible hitters as well—not hitting homers, just getting tons of hits.

WORDS to KNOW

On deck: The batter who is scheduled to hit next is considered to be waiting "on deck." Usually there is an on-deck circle where the player stands and takes practice swings.

FUN FACT

League Championship Series

The National League and the American League each have a championship series to see who goes to the World Series. The NLCS and ALCS are both played in early October. They began in 1969 when the leagues were broken into divisions, and used to be a best-of-five game series. Today they are a best-of-seven game series.

Hard Ball

Baseball is a game full of action and larger than life characters. Fill in as many wild words as you can, using the across and down clues. We left you some T-O-U-G-H letters as hints!

Across

3. A fun baseball game that two people can play against an upright surface.
6. Team name: Pittsburgh _____.
7. The nickname for a powerful hitter.
11. The smooth, round stick used to hit a baseball.
13. The 37-foot-high wall in Boston's Fenway Park.
16. A "_____ hitter" is a hitter who hits for someone else.
17. A player will "_____" a base by running from one base to another before the next player at bat has hit the ball.
19. Team Name: San Francisco _____.
21. If the hitter bunts with a man on third base, it's called a "_____ play."

Down

1. One of Joe DiMaggio's nicknames was "_____'n Joe."
2. When a hitter stops getting hits for a while.
4. Hank Aaron's nickname was "The _____."
5. "The _____" is when fans in the bleachers stand up and then sit while moving their arms up and down in a motion that goes all around the stadium.
6. A "_____" fly is a ball that goes high up in the air and is easily caught by an infield player.
7. The sharp bumps on the bottom of baseball player's shoes.
8. "The Seventh Inning _____" gives fans a chance to get up and move around after sitting for a long time.
9. Team name: Los Angeles _____.
10. The score made by a player who touches first, second, third, and home base.
11. Jose Canseco and Mark McGwire were known as the "_____ Brothers."
12. A ball hit out of fair territory.
14. A _____ play is when a player is trapped between two bases. He has to scramble to get to one base or the other before being tagged out.
15. A "_____ ball" is the speediest pitch that a pitcher can throw.
18. A player will sometimes have to _____ headfirst into a base to avoid being tagged out.
20. A "grand _____" is a home run hit when the bases are loaded.

26

FUN FACT

Bucky

At the end of the 1978 season the Yankees and the Red Sox were tied for first place in the American League Eastern Division. A one-game playoff would determine who the winner would be. The Yankees shortstop, Bucky Dent, who hit just five home runs all season, would hit the biggest homer of his career to help send the Yankees to the American League Championship Playoffs . . . and the World Series.

There was some great pitching as well from Sandy Koufax, Bob Gibson, Juan Marichal, Jim Palmer, and Tom Seaver, all of whom would end up in the Hall of Fame.

Baseball continued to expand, with four more teams added in 1969, the Montreal Expos and San Diego Padres in the National League and the Seattle Pilots and Kansas City Royals in the American League. The leagues now had 12 teams each and were split into two 6-team divisions, East and West. Now you're probably wondering what happened to those terrible Mets. Well, after being pretty dreadful for seven years, they shocked the world in 1969. The same year that men landed on the moon for the first time ever, the Mets beat the Baltimore Orioles in five games to win the World Series.

1970–1979

The 1970s had people wearing bell bottoms and dancing to disco. It was a time for many baseball firsts. In 1972 the Major League Baseball players went on strike for the first time ever. Also in 1972 Major League Baseball had their first ever female umpire. In 1973 the American League would have the first ever "designated hitter"—a hitter who bats for the pitcher, still used today. In 1974 the great slugger Hank Aaron would become the first player to surpass the 714 all-time home runs hit by Babe Ruth. Aaron began the 1974 season needing only one to tie Ruth and two to pass him. Everyone interested in baseball, and even people who weren't fans, waited for the big moment. Early in the season, on April 8, Aaron hit the historic home run to put him first in what is probably the most significant individual record in sports, All-Time Home Runs. He would go on to finish his career where he began it, in Milwaukee (except it was now with the Brewers), with 755 homers—a record that still stands today.

In 1975 there was another important first. Frank Robinson became baseball's first African-American manager. In 1977 Lou Brock became the first player ever to steal 900 bases, as he took over Ty Cobb's all-time mark of 892. Rickey Henderson has since passed them both.

Besides the many firsts, baseball in the 1970s saw many new stadiums featuring artificial turf. Balls took high bounces and fielders had to adjust so the ball didn't bounce over their heads. Base stealing became more popular than ever, and relief pitching became a more important part of the game as managers began using relievers more and more often.

The mid-1970s were dominated by the Oakland A's, who won three World Series titles in a row with Reggie Jackson and Rollie Fingers. Then came the Yankees in the late '70s, and by 1979 the Orioles were on top with 102 wins. The National League belonged to the Phillies and the Pirates in the east and the Dodgers and the Big Red Machine in Cincinnati out west, featuring Pete Rose, Johnny Bench, Joe Morgan, George Foster, and Junior's dad, Ken Griffey Sr.

Other superstars of the '70s included Willie Stargell, Lou Brock, Tony Oliva, Rod Carew, Steve Garvey, Eddie Murray, Thurman Munson, Steve Carlton, Tom Seaver, Jim Palmer, and strikeout king Nolan Ryan.

1980–1989

VCRs were becoming popular, personal computers were on their way, and free agency, which had begun in the 1970s, was the new term in baseball in the early '80s. For many years players who were signed to a team had to play for that team until they were traded or released. Now, with free agency, players were only tied to a team until their contract with that

About Broadcasting

Phil Rizzuto, the great Yankee shortstop of the 1950s and Hall of Famer, became a broadcaster with the Yankees after retiring. Rizzuto once said: "I like radio better than television because if you make a mistake on radio, they don't know. You can make up anything on the radio."

Designated Hitter:
A designated hitter is a player who bats for the pitcher. The American League has designated hitters and the National League does not—NL pitchers bat for themselves.

team ended. Then they could become free agents and go to whatever team gave them the most money. There was much more involved in sorting out how free agency worked. Players and owners didn't agree, so baseball players went on strike in the middle of the 1981 season. Over 700 games were cancelled and when baseball finally returned, the season was split into two halves. The winners of the first half played the winners of the second half in a special playoff series. Fans were not very happy with baseball, and many did not come back to see the games after the strike.

Suddenly money became more important than statistics, and all people talked about were ballplayers now making one million dollars a year, an incredible amount of money, especially considering that Babe Ruth, probably the greatest player ever, never made more than $80,000.

There was some on-field excitement, too, as Cal Ripken Jr. began a career with the Baltimore Orioles that will land him in the Hall of Fame when he retires. Singles and doubles hitters Don Mattingly and Wade Boggs battled as the two top American League hitters, while Tony Gwynn was alone atop the National League in batting average. Mike Schmidt, Andre Dawson, and Dave Winfield were among the slugging stars. Jose Canseco and Mark McGwire would emerge on the scene, with McGwire hitting 49 homers as a rookie for the Oakland A's. Although not yet a star, Barry Bonds would also start off playing his first seasons with the Pirates.

Family Affair

At one time, Cal Ripken Jr. and his brother Billy played on the same team, the Baltimore Orioles, with their dad as a coach. That's a family act.

1990–1999

The 1990s started off on the wrong foot. In 1990 the owners locked the players out of spring training. Unlike a strike where the players walk out, the owners called a halt to their own teams' spring training. After a settlement was reached, the season began—better late than never. The Reds handed it to the Oakland A's in 1990 to win the World Series. Then, the National League became the Atlanta Braves' League. For the rest of the 1990s the Braves, led by the great pitching of Greg Maddux and Tom Glavine were the best team in the league, making the playoffs or World Series every year, but only winning one World Series title.

Baseball was rolling along in the early 1990s, but in 1994 things went sour. Just after the leagues decided to split into three divisions rather than two, more important things had to be figured out. The players and the owners went to war over money, and a strike ended the 1994 baseball season in August. It was the first time since 1904 that there was no post season, no World Series, and no championship team. Millionaire players and millionaire team owners got very little sympathy from the fans who were deprived of watching and enjoying their favorite game. When baseball returned in 1995, attendance was way down. For the next couple of seasons many fans were turned off to baseball.

There was one shining moment, and that came in 1995 when Cal Ripken Jr. of the Orioles set a record by playing in his 2,131st consecutive game, breaking the record set by Lou Gehrig in 1939. The September 6 game drew a sellout crowd, which included the president of the United States, plus millions of fans who watched on TV around the world.

In 1997 baseball owners decided that they'd try to draw fans back by starting interleague play, which meant regular season games between National and American league teams.

All-Star Game History

The first All-Star game was played in 1933. The American League won 12 of the first 16 All-Star games before things turned around, and the National League won 11 of 16 starting in the 1950s.

All-Star Fun Fact

The only grand slam home run in an All-Star game came in 1983 and was hit by Boston Red Sox slugger Fred Lynn. The American League won 13 to 3.

All-Star Fact

There was no All-Star game in 1945 because of World War II. It was the only year since it began in 1933 that the All-Star game was called off.

FUN FACT

All-Star Fun Fact

In the second All-Star game ever played, in 1934, "King" Carl Hubbell, the ace of the Giants pitching staff started the game for the National League. In the bottom of the first, Hubbell allowed a lead-off single and then a walk. He would then face Babe Ruth, Lou Gehrig, Jimmie Foxx, and Al Simmons, four future Hall of Famers who would retire with a combined 2,048 home runs and .330+ batting average. Hubbell, also a future Hall of Famer, reared back and fired away. Down went Ruth on strikes, down went Gehrig on strikes, and it was the same for Jimmie Foxx. In the next inning Hubbell struck out Al Simmons and added a strikeout to another of the game's feared hitters, Joe Cronin, giving him five straight strikeouts in a row of five of the greatest hitters of all time. It still stands as one of the greatest All-Star game accomplishments.

Longtime baseball fans weren't happy about it, but on June 12, 1997, the Texas Rangers and San Francisco Giants played in the first interleague game. What at first appeared to be a novelty caught on as cross-town rivals like the Cubs and White Sox in Chicago, The A's and Giants in neighboring Oakland and San Francisco, and the Mets and Yankees in New York all faced each other during the season.

But it wasn't interleague play that gave the game the shot in the arm it needed. It was the amazing home run battle of 1998 that brought fans back to the ballpark and to their TV sets to watch baseball. The Cardinals' Mark McGwire, coming off a 58-home run season, the Cubs' Sammy Sosa, and the Mariners' Ken Griffey Jr. started hitting home runs at a tremendous pace. Day by day all season long the three sluggers kept pounding out home runs. Over time, Griffey fell behind, but by late August it was clear that both Sosa and McGwire had a great shot at breaking the record of 61 home runs set by Roger Maris in 1961. On September 7, in St. Louis, McGwire did it, he hit home run number 61 in the 144th game of the year. Then on September 8 in front of another packed house and worldwide TV audience, McGwire hit number 62. The celebration was tremendous, and McGwire became a sports legend. By the final weekend of the season, not only did McGwire have 66 home runs, but so did Sosa. Who would win the battle? McGwire hit four home runs over the next two ball games and ended up with a new record of 70 home runs. Wow!

The 2000 Season

The 2000 baseball season provided plenty of excitement with hitters like Jason Giambi of the Oakland A's (AL MVP) and Troy Glaus of the Anaheim Angels (AL home run champion) becoming two of the biggest young home run stars in the

American League. Todd Helton of the Rockies tore up the National League with an incredible season. It was yet another amazing season for Red Sox star Pedro Martinez, who led the major leagues with a 1.57 ERA. It was also the year that saw the first Subway (World) Series in over 40 years played between the New York Mets and the New York Yankees. Fans could take the #7 train to Shea Stadium or the #4 train to Yankee Stadium, hence the name "Subway Series."

There was a lot of excitement all around New York City in October as the two teams squared off in a series that saw five close, well-pitched games, all decided by one or two runs. After an extra-inning win in game #1 by the Yankees and a great pitching performance by Roger Clemens to win game #2, the Mets rallied to win game #3 and make it a 2-1 series, in favor of the Yankees. Then the Yankees won the final two close games to win the series 4-1. It was their third championship season in a row. They were honored with a ticker tape parade in Manhattan.

Baseball Today

Many stars of the 1990s were still going strong as we entered the new millenium, including Barry Bonds, Jeff Bagwell, Barry Larkin, Greg Maddux, Randy Johnson, the all-time base stealer Rickey Henderson, plus McGwire, Sosa, and Griffey. New superstars have emerged on the scene, including Mike Piazza, Juan Gonzalez, Chipper Jones, Pedro Martinez, Alex Rodriguez, and others. The salaries are out of this world, and so are the home run totals as baseballs keep flying out of the ballparks.

Baseball today is seeing a lot of great hitting and many pitchers trying to tame the big sluggers. Cable television

Baseball Q & A: The Minor Leagues

Each major league team has several minor league teams. They are organized by different levels. Rookie League and A Teams are for the newest players signed by teams from college or high school. Then players work their way up to AA minor league teams and finally to AAA minor league teams, which are one (big) step away from the major leagues. Almost every player spends a few years in the minors before coming to the major leagues. Some players are sent back down to the minor leagues if they are not playing well at the major league level, and sometimes a good major league player will go to the minors after an injury to get used to playing again and to make sure they can play again without any pain. Minor league teams are in many smaller cities across the country, and games can be fun to watch—and you can usually get good seats. Sometimes you'll see a great player up close before he makes it to the pros.

Paige on Age

Negro Leagues star and former major league pitcher, Satchel Paige, who pitched for nearly 30 years and even appeared in a major league game at the age of 59, once said, "Age is a case of mind over matter. If you don't mind, it don't matter."

makes it possible for you to watch games from all over the country. ESPN and other networks carry up-to-the minute scores and information, which is also available on the Internet. Teams even have their own Web sites.

Several new stadiums opened to start the new century, and others are being built. The game is enjoying a great deal of interest, but there is some concern as salaries go up, up, up. Can teams from smaller cities (called smaller markets) such as Pittsburgh, Kansas City, Montreal, or San Diego compete with teams from New York, Atlanta, or Los Angeles, which have more money to pay millions and millions of dollars to free agents? Only time will tell what will happen to the many teams who can't afford these big talents. In the meantime, baseball remains a great game to watch and enjoy.

The Negro Leagues

The National League was formed in 1876, and in the early years of baseball there was no color barrier. In fact, Moses Fleetwood joined the Toledo ballclub in 1884 as the first professional African-American ballplayer, and others followed. These players, however, were treated badly by fans, opposing players, and their own teammates. Besides calling them names, white pitchers would often throw what are called knockdown pitches aimed at the batter's head to knock him down. Little by little as 1900 approached, there were fewer and fewer African-American players in baseball. There was no written rule, but owners just no longer signed African-American players.

Since it was becoming impossible to get into the major leagues, African-American players began forming their own teams in the 1890s. By the early 1900s the teams were playing

independently all over the eastern part of the United States in cities like New York and Philadelphia. Often these teams played exhibition games against major league teams, and they did well. It was obvious that many of the players on these teams had the talent to play in the major leagues, but the practice of discrimination by race was too strong, and they did not break into the all-white major leagues.

One great pitcher of the early 1900s was Rube Foster, who pitched for the 1906 Philadelphia Giants, an independent African-American ballclub. He would go on to be the founder of the Negro Leagues, which began in 1920 with eight teams. In 1923, Foster helped start a second league, which began with six new teams.

There were problems in these leagues, such as finding places to play. Often the teams had to rent stadiums from white owners, who didn't always treat them fairly. Many owners did not allow them to use the "white" locker rooms. Nonetheless, the teams persisted, with players playing for the love of the game more than anything else, since most were not making much money.

The 1930s, however, marked the end of the early Negro Leagues because of the Depression, which hit the entire nation very hard. Most of the teams, which had a hard time making money, had to call it quits. There were, however, some teams that managed to play—touring teams such as the Pittsburgh Crawfords and the Homestead Grays. Many major leaguers had great respect for the African-American ballplayers and still played exhibition games against these touring teams.

By the late 1930s the Negro Leagues were back with new teams. Satchel Paige was perhaps the greatest legend of the Negro Leagues. He was a star pitcher in the 1930s for the Kansas City Monarchs. He would eventually make the major leagues with the Cleveland Indians in 1948 at the age of 42

FUN FACT

All-Star Injury Fest

The first All-Star game of the new century saw the National League with an incredible starting team that included Barry Bonds, Mark McGwire, Sammy Sosa, Ken Griffey Jr., and Mike Piazza. But by the day of the game, Bonds, McGwire, Griffey, and Piazza were all injured—plus Greg Maddux and three prominent American Leaguers, including Cal Ripken, who had played in 16 straight All-Star games, and Alex Rodriguez.

Generations

Imagine playing in the major leagues just like your father and grandfather. Three times it has been done. One family is still going strong today. The Boone family has seen Ray Boone, his son Bob Boone, and his two grandsons Brett and Aaron Boone all play in the major leagues. Brett and Aaron are still playing today.

FUN FACT

The Case of the Missing RBI

For many years, Hack Wilson of the Cubs had the record for the most runs batted in in one season—190. However, someone looking over old baseball records many years later and long after Wilson died discovered that he was not given an RBI that he was entitled to during that season. So, now the record is actually 191.

and pitch for a few years, then return to pitch three scoreless innings for the Kansas City Athletics in 1968 at the age of 59. To get an idea of how good Satchel Paige really was, he once faced a Cubs player in an exhibition game who made comments that he didn't think Satchel's Negro League team or Satchel was really very good. So, when the player came to bat, Paige took his fielders off the field and told them they could go sit down in the dugout. Paige wasn't clowning, but proving a point. He proceeded to pitch with no one on the field to help him get the hitter out. He struck the batter out on three pitches.

In the 1940s a team in Brooklyn, the Brooklyn Brown Bombers, was owned by Dodgers president and general manager Branch Rickey. Rickey was determined, despite the feelings of the other team owners, to scout and sign baseball's first African-American major leaguer. In 1946 it was Rickey who watched the Kansas City Monarchs come to town with a young player named Jackie Robinson. Rickey signed Robinson to a minor league contract, and the rest is history, as he would break the "color barrier" and become baseball's first African-American player of the twentieth century.

As more and more African-American players made the major leagues, there was no need for the Negro Leagues. While many of the greatest Negro League stars never made it to the major leagues, the leagues served a purpose in giving these ballplayers a place to show their great talents and play the game they loved. It would eventually serve as a showcase for players to get to the major leagues. It is only unfortunate that it took so many years for it to happen.

Ballclubs on the Move

Many of the major league teams today played in other cities, or had different names in the past. Below is a fun list of just some of the former names and former homes of the teams we know today. *Bet your friends won't know most of these former team names!*

- The Oakland Athletics (also called the A's) had two previous homes. They played in Kansas City from 1955 to 1967, and before that they were the Philadelphia Athletics.

- The New York Yankees were known as the Highlanders from 1903 to 1912. Before the American League was officially started, they played in Baltimore as the Baltimore Orioles in 1901 and 1902. The Orioles we know today weren't around yet.

- The Minnesota Twins were the Washington Senators from 1901 to 1960. After they moved, a new Washington Senators team was formed in 1961. Unfortunately for the baseball fans of Washington, they also moved and became the Texas Rangers.

- The Cleveland Indians were always in Cleveland. However, between 1901 and 1914 they kept changing their name. They were the Blues, the Broncos, and the Naps before becoming the Indians in 1915.

- The Boston Red Sox, like the Indians, never moved, but had a hard time finding a name they liked. Between 1901 and 1906 they were known as the Somersets, the Pilgrims, and the Puritans before becoming the Red Sox in 1907.

- The Baltimore Orioles that we know today came into being in 1955 after moving from St Louis, where they were the Browns from 1902 through 1954.

(continued)

Ballclubs on the Move (continued)

- The Atlanta Braves have a long history dating back to 1876 and covering three cities. Prior to moving to Atlanta, they were the Milwaukee Braves from 1953 to 1965. Before that they were in Boston for 59 years. They were the Red Caps, the Beaneaters, the Doves, the Pilgrims, and on two different occasions the Bees.

- The Cubs have always been in Chicago, at least since 1876, but also saw a few name changes in the 1800s, including the White Stockings, Orphans, and Colts.

- The Reds, the oldest major league team still in existence, dating back to 1869, were originally the Red Stockings. They became the Reds as far back as 1880, then changed their name briefly to the Red Legs in the 1950s. Realizing how silly that sounded, they went back to Reds.

- The Los Angeles Dodgers were until 1957 the Brooklyn Dodgers, also known as the Robins from 1914 to 1931.

- The San Francisco Giants were until 1957 the New York Giants.

- The Houston Astros were the Houston Colt 45s for their first three seasons, from 1962 to 1964.

- The Milwaukee Brewers were the Seattle Pilots in 1969 before moving to Milwaukee in their second season. In the late 1990s they also moved from the American to the National League.

- The Philadelphia Phillies changed their name to the Blue Jays for the 1944 and 1945 seasons before changing it back to Phillies.

Inning 3

The Greats
of the Game

FUN FACT

The Cy Young Award

The Cy Young Award, named after the pitcher with the most wins in baseball history, and obviously one of the greatest ever, is given each year to the best pitchers in each league.

Pitchers

Pitchers are sometimes called "hurlers." Successful major league pitchers fire baseballs at 90 to 100 miles per hour and have mastered a few types of pitches. They also must have good control, meaning they hit the strike zone more often than not and don't walk too many batters.

Over the years, there have been changes in pitching in the major leagues. Pitchers used to start ball games and very often pitch all nine innings. Today a "complete game," where a pitcher goes all nine innings, is very rare. Pitchers would also start games every three or four days, which over the years has become every five days. In the early 1900s pitchers would win 30 games or more in a season, but by the 1930s, and ever since, 20 wins has become the mark to shoot for in a season. Today, only a few pitchers win 20 games in a year.

Pitchers' earned run averages (ERA), telling the average number of runs they allow in a game, have also gone up over the years. Through most of the 1900s, an earned run average under 3.00 per game was excellent, and between 3.00 and 4.00 was very good. Today, only a few pitchers have ERAs under 4.00. In the early and even the mid-1900s, the only time a relief pitcher was called in was if the starting pitcher was doing poorly. Over the past 30 years this has changed, and relief pitchers now come into games much more often. It's not unusual to see three or four pitchers in a game.

The game has changed over the years, but the basic idea that the pitcher wants to get the batter out remains the same. Below are just a few of

the all-time greats. Ask your parents or your grandparents about them; they may have seen them pitch.

Listed below each pitcher are his career wins (W), losses (L), Earned Run Average (ERA), and strikeouts (K's). Also listed are the teams on which they spent the majority of their careers. Keep in mind that only 20 pitchers have won 300 or more games and only 12 pitchers have 3,000 or more career strikeouts in modern baseball history (since 1903).

Southpaw: A left-handed pitcher is sometimes referred to as a southpaw.

Steve Carlton Cardinals, Phillies

W–L	ERA	K
329–244	3.22	4,176

They just called him "Lefty," because many considered him the greatest lefty to ever pitch. Carlton came up in 1965, and in 1971 he won 20 games for the first time in his career. Surprisingly, he was then traded to the Phillies, where in 1972 he won 27 games and had an earned run average of 1.97, leading the league. He also had over 300 strikeouts that year and won the coveted Cy Young Award in 1972 as the best pitcher in the National League. He won the award three more times in his long career. By the time Carlton retired he was the ninth all-time pitcher in wins, and he still ranks second all-time in strikeouts. Although he never liked to talk with sportswriters very much and kept to himself, the baseball writers had no problem voting this great pitcher into the Hall of Fame in 1994.

Carlton K's

Carlton once struck out 19 batters in a game, which at the time was a major league record. As is the case with many records, it has since been broken.

Dennis Eckersley Red Sox, Indians, Cubs, Athletics, Cardinals

W–L	ERA	K
197–171	3.50	2,401

For many years, relief pitching in major league baseball meant the starter was doing poorly and the manager would have to go to a "lesser" pitcher who was a reliever. It wasn't

Picture This #3

This combination of pictures "spells" a well known baseball play.

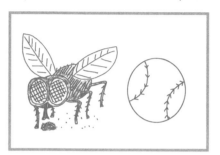

until the 1960s that relief pitching became a big part of the game. Eckersly was one of the greatest relievers of the past 30 years, if not the greatest, in a group that included Rollie Fingers, Lee Smith, Sparky Lyle, and several others. Originally a starter and even a 20-game winner in the 1970s, "Eck" would become a relief pitcher in 1987 and a full-time closer in 1988. He was amazing! In 1990 his ERA was 0.60. More incredible than that was that in two full seasons combined he walked only seven batters. Between 1988 and 1992 he saved 230 games for the A's, totally baffling opposing hitters. One can only imagine how many saves he could have had if he had been a closer for all of his seemingly endless 23-year career. Eckersley retired in 1998 and should make the Hall of Fame in 2003.

Bob Feller Indians

W–L	ERA	K
266–162	3.25	2,561

Bob Feller made it to the major leagues in 1936, before his eighteenth birthday. He grew up on a farm in Iowa and became one of the hardest throwing pitchers of all time, firing fastballs of nearly 100 miles per hour and earning the nickname "Rapid Robert." He would lead the league in strikeouts seven times during his career. He won 20 games six times and 266 games in his career and would have easily won at least 325 had it not been for World War II. Feller did not wait to be drafted into the army. Instead, at age 23 he left an all-star baseball career to serve his country by enlisting in the Navy for four years. Feller went from the ballpark to an American battleship. In 1946, he returned to the Indians and to the cheers of the fans who had waited for him and were very proud of him for doing what he believed in, serving his country. Feller retired at the age of 38 and made the Hall of Fame in 1962.

Lefty Grove Athletics, Red Sox

W–L	ERA	K
300–141	3.06	2,266

Grove was 25 when he made the majors with the Philadelphia Athletics. By his third season he was a 20-game winner, and by 1931 he would go 31–4 while winning the Most Valuable Player Award (MVP). In his seven years with the A's Grove was, in a word, "awesome." He led the league in ERA four times, while posting a record of 172 wins and only 41 losses between 1927 and 1933. After a total of nine ERA titles, Grove retired in 1941 ending a 17-year career. During his best years, Grove was as tough a pitcher to hit against as anyone who ever pitched. He won 68 percent of his games and made the Hall of Fame in 1947.

Walter Johnson Senators

W–L	ERA	K
416–279	2.16	3,509

Nicknamed "The Big Train," Walter Johnson was very possibly the greatest pitcher ever. Johnson did everything well: he threw hard, had control, threw a lot of innings, and never seemed to get tired. He came up with the Washington Senators in 1907 at only 19 years of age and began a 21-year career that was truly remarkable. Johnson won 20 or more games per season 10 years in a row, led the league in strike-outs 12 times and in ERA five times, including a 1.14 ERA in 1913 when he won 36 games. His 416 wins is second best of all time and his 110 career shutouts the most ever. He never won a Cy Young Award since Cy was also still pitching, and the award didn't exist yet. He did, however, win the Most Valuable Player Award on a couple of occasions. Johnson was one of the first five players selected to the Hall of Fame in 1936.

WORDS to KNOW

Save: When a pitcher comes into a close ball-game and gets the final outs it is called a save.

Lots of Wins!

Did you know that the great Walter Johnson actually won 946 games? He won 416 as a pitcher and a 530 as a manager.

Sandy Koufax Dodgers

W–L	ERA	K
165–87	2.76	2,396

Sandy Koufax was born in Brooklyn in 1935 and by the age of 19 was pitching for the hometown favorites, the Brooklyn Dodgers. He was part of the team that picked up in 1957 and moved away to Los Angeles. An average pitcher during his first several seasons, he just got better and better and led the league in strikeouts in 1961. By 1963, major league hitters considered him the toughest pitcher in baseball. He posted 25 wins, struck out over 300, and led the league with an ERA of 1.88. He not only won the Cy Young Award as the best pitcher but the Most Valuable Player Award as well. Over the next four years, he would win three more Cy Young Awards, leading the league in wins, strikeouts, and ERA each year. He also threw four no-hitters. Unfortunately, Koufax developed serious arthritis in his elbow and by 1967, at the top of his game, was forced to retire. In 1972 he was elected to the Hall of Fame at only 37 years of age. Koufax did not pitch in the major leagues for very long, but he was definitely one of the best in baseball history.

Christy Mathewson Giants

W–L	ERA	K
373–188	2.13	2,502

Watching pitchers today struggle to keep an ERA under 4.00, it seems almost impossible to imagine that Christy Mathewson could pitch for 17 years and post a 2.13 career earned run average. Mathewson made the major leagues at the age of 20 in the year 1900. In 1901 he would pick up his first of 373 career wins. Back in those days pitchers threw a lot of innings, and Mathewson topped 300 innings pitched for 11 seasons. Giants manager John McGraw figured, why not let him

pitch a lot, he was almost impossible to score on. Mathewson rattled off a string of 12 consecutive 20+ win seasons with a high of 37 in 1908. He was the National League's best pitcher for the first decade of the twentieth century. In 1939 he was one of the first five players ever to be elected to the Hall of Fame with Ruth, Cobb, Wagner, and Johnson.

Nolan Ryan Mets, Angels, Astros, Rangers

W–L	ERA	K
324–292	3.19	5,386

There are few athletes that can match the accomplishments of Nolan Ryan. He was truly a flamethrower, firing the ball harder and faster than anyone had ever seen. When Ryan came up with the Mets in 1966 he could throw very hard but had control problems and walked a lot of hitters. In 1972 the Mets traded him to the California Angels, and there he turned into a big winner and became the king of strikeouts. He would lead the league 11 times in strikeouts, once having as many as 383 in a season. While most pitchers would be thrilled to throw one no-hitter in their career, Ryan would also set a major league record by throwing seven . . . that's right, seven! A native of Texas, Ryan was excited when he got to play for the Houston Astros, where he topped Walter Johnson's long-held all-time career strikeout record in 1983 at the age of 36. Ryan, however, was far from done. Somehow, no matter how hard he threw his arm never seemed to get tired. He surprised everyone by pitching in the big leagues for another 10 years and retired at age 46. By that time he had over 5,000 strikeouts, far more than anyone else. He made the Hall of Fame in 1999.

The Ryan Express

"You can't hit what you can't see," was the familiar complaint of batters who struck out time and time again trying to hit a Nolan Ryan fastball, which became known as "The Ryan Express."

WORDS to KNOW

Rain Out: A rain out is when a game is called off because of rain. If this happens before the fifth inning, the game doesn't count. If it's after the fifth inning it's considered an official game, and whichever team was ahead at the time wins.

Tom Seaver Mets, Reds, White Sox, Yankees, Red Sox

W–L	ERA	K
311–205	2.86	3,640

When "Tom Terrific" came up with the New York Mets in 1967, the Mets were the worst team in the major leagues. By 1969, they shocked everyone and won 100 games, with Tom Seaver winning 25 of them on the way to a World Championship. Seaver won his first of three Cy Young Awards that year and became the heart and soul of the Mets. In 1973 he led the Mets back to the World Series, but this time they lost to the A's. When he was traded away in 1977 Mets fans were very upset, but Reds fans were excited. After some successful years in Cincinnati, he returned to the Mets for a short time in 1983, but it was near the end of his long career. Tom won 20 or more games four times and lead the league in strikeouts five times. Seaver retired as one of the 20 winningest pitchers of all time and sits fourth all-time in strikeouts. He was elected to the Hall of Fame in 1992 and even after that returned to the Mets one more time, only this time as an announcer in their broadcasting booth.

Cy Young Indians, Browns, Red Sox

W–L	ERA	K
511–315	2.63	2,800

You'll have a very hard time finding anyone who saw Cy Young pitch, since he was born in 1867 and his career spanned from 1890 to 1911. Nicknamed "Cyclone" because of how hard he threw, he must have been quite amazing, since the award given to the best pitchers every year in baseball is called the Cy Young Award. Even though the game was different and pitchers threw more innings in Cy's time, he was still pretty amazing. His 511 wins and 7,377 innings pitched are by far the most ever and will probably never be topped. Young threw three no-hitters during his career and once had 44 consecutive scoreless

innings. He completed nearly 750 games, or almost 34 per season. To give you an idea of how much he pitched, consider that today the best pitchers throw maybe six or seven complete games in a season. Needless to say, he was elected into the Hall of Fame in 1937. He died in 1955, and in 1956, in his honor, the Cy Young Award was established for the best pitcher each year in baseball.

Hitters

It's hard to find anyone who doesn't like to pick up a bat and swing at a ball to see where they can hit it. The basic idea of hitting hasn't changed all that much over the years. The type of hits changed in the 1920s from mostly singles and doubles to plenty of home runs, thanks to Babe Ruth. Even with more home runs, the best major league ballplayers aimed for a batting average of over .300. In the early part of the twentieth century some hitters would top .400, but fielders wore smaller gloves, which may have been part of the reason for such high averages. No one has hit over .400 in the major leagues since Ted Williams in 1941. In the late 1960s there were fewer .300 hitters, and pitchers dominated the game. By the 1990s, however, hitters began bulking up and working out to build up their strength. Today home runs are flying out of ballparks at an amazing rate, and there are plenty of hitters batting well into the high .300s.

Over the years there have been many great hitters, but only a few managed to hit, run, and field at the highest level for many years. Many of the superstars featured here not only hit for power but stole bases, and most importantly, they were the guys you could count on when you needed the big hit to win a game. These are just a few of the game's biggest superstars and most popular all-time favorites.

FUN FACT

Shhh!

Perhaps Cy Young wouldn't want to mention it, but besides the most wins ever, he also holds the record for the most losses ever at 315. Of course, that's because he played more games than any other pitcher!

The Envelope, Please

The first Cy Young Award was given to Don Newcombe of the Dodgers in 1956. From 1956 through 1966 only one pitcher in the major leagues was given the award. Starting in 1967, one pitcher in each league received a Cy Young Award.

Brothers

There have been a lot of brothers to play baseball. Do you know which brother combination hit the most home runs? Hank and Tommie Aaron. Hammerin' Hank hit 755, while Tommie added on just 13 for a total of 768.

Under each hitter is his career home run total (HR), runs batted in total (RBI), and batting average (BA). Only 16 players have topped 500 home runs, while 1,500 runs batted in, 3,000 hits, and a career average over .300 are all benchmark totals of the best players in the game.

Henry Aaron Braves, Brewers

HR	RBI	BA
755	2,297	.305

Many people thought Babe Ruth's record of 714 career home runs might never be broken. Hank Aaron, nicknamed "The Hammer," had another idea. Aaron played briefly in the Negro Leagues before being signed in 1954 by the Milwaukee Braves, who would move to Atlanta in 1966.

Aaron never topped 50 in a season, but belted at least 25 home runs 18 times, with a high of 47. He would also post over 120 RBIs seven times while setting the all-time career RBI record. By the time he finished his 23-year career, back in Milwaukee as a member of the Brewers, he was also near the top in games played, hits, runs scored, and doubles. Aaron made the Hall of Fame in 1982.

Johnny Bench Reds

HR	RBI	BA
389	1,376	.267

There was never a greater catcher than Johnny Bench. He broke into the major leagues at 20 years old in style, making the All-Star game and winning Rookie of the Year honors. In 1970, his third season, Bench won the National League MVP with 45 homers and 148 RBIs while leading the Reds to the World Series. Bench would top the 100 RBI mark on five occasions as the main cog in Cincinnati's "Big Red Machine," the nickname for the Reds great team of the '70s.

Besides his tremendous power hitting and many clutch hits, Bench was also an incredible defensive catcher with a great throwing arm. He would win 10 Gold Glove Awards as the best defensive catcher in the National League until injuries forced him to spend more time at third and first base. Two World Championships and his consistent play made Johnny Bench a household name as one of baseball's most popular players of the 1970s. The injuries from catching, however, caught up with him, and by age 35 Bench had to call it quits. In 1989 he was elected to the Hall of Fame.

Roberto Clemente Pirates

HR	RBI	BA
240	1,305	.317

Clemente was a tremendous all-around ballplayer. He not only could hit for a high average, but he had power and was a super defensive outfielder, winning 12 Gold Gloves. He joined the Pirates in the mid-1950s as a 20-year-old rookie from Puerto Rico. He would go on to become the greatest player from Puerto Rico and the first Hispanic player elected to the Hall of Fame. Four times in the 1960s Clemente led the league in batting, and four times he had over 200 hits in a season. He appeared in two World Series for the Pirates and batted .362 overall, helping lead the Pirates to the title in 1971. Clemente became one of the few players to get his 3,000th hit, which came at the end of the 1972 season. It would be his last hit ever. On New Year's Eve of that year he was on his way to deliver supplies to victims of a severe earthquake in Nicaragua when the plane he was on crashed. Clemente died at age 38 but is remembered as a hero both on and off the field.

Ty Cobb Tigers, Athletics

HR	RBI	BA
118	1,961	.357

Cobb was one of the toughest players of all time. He worked very hard and spent hours practicing hitting, sliding, and throwing while on his way to the major leagues in 1905 at the age of 18. The hard work paid off. Cobb played 24 years, almost all for the Tigers, and hit under .300 just once, as a rookie. In fact, he batted over .400 three times and led the league in batting average 12 times on his way to an incredible all-time high .367 career batting average. Not only was he a great hitter, but Cobb was one of the best base stealers ever, stealing nearly 900 bases. Cobb's great hitting made him one of the first five players elected to the Hall of Fame. The fans enjoyed watching Cobb play, but he rarely got along with his teammates, and opposing players hated him. He would sharpen his spikes before the game and then slide in hard, feet first. Cobb would later say when he was older that if he had one thing to do differently it would be to have had more friends.

Manager, Too

Cobb not only played for the Tigers, but for six years was a player manager for them, too, winning 479 games and losing 444, taking the Tigers as high as second place.

Joe DiMaggio Yankees

HR	RBI	BA
361	1,537	.325

"Joltin' Joe" and "The Yankee Clipper" were two nicknames for the great Yankee center fielder of the 1930s and '40s. He was as popular and well liked on and off the field as any baseball player ever. The most valuable player in 1941, DiMaggio not only hit .351 while driving in 125 runs, but he only struck out 13 times! DiMaggio's marvelous career is highlighted by his amazing streak of getting a hit in 56 consecutive games. No one has come within a dozen games of matching that mark set 50 years ago. Three years spent in the army and injuries limited

DiMaggio to only 13 years in the big leagues, but, he helped lead the Yankees to the World Series 10 times in those 13 seasons. He was elected to the Hall of Fame in 1955. DiMaggio remained famous for many years after playing baseball. He married legendary movie actress Marilyn Monroe, owned a popular restaurant in San Francisco, did many TV commercials, was mentioned in the novel *The Old Man and the Sea*, and in the hit song "Mrs. Robinson." "Joltin' Joe" certainly was a legend.

Jimmie Foxx Athletics, Red Sox

HR	RBI	BA
534	1,922	.325

The "Double X" they called him, and he was one of the most feared hitters of the 1920s and '30s. Playing in the shadow of "The Babe" and Lou Gehrig, Foxx was slugging over 30 homers a year for 12 consecutive seasons, hitting 58 in 1932 while winning the Triple Crown. He also topped the 100 RBI mark 13 straight years, with totals as high as 169 and 175. Even though Foxx led the A's to three pennants, manager Connie Mack didn't want to pay him more money in 1935. In fact, he tried to cut Foxx's salary. Foxx would not play for less money and was sent to the Red Sox where he continued to clobber American League pitching before playing briefly for the Cubs and Phillies at the end of his 20-year career. Foxx was a dominant hitter and one of the biggest stars of the '20s and '30s, respected by everyone in baseball. He was elected to the Hall of Fame in 1951.

Lou Gehrig Yankees

HR	RBI	BA
493	1,995	.340

He was called the Iron Horse because he was always in the lineup. Gehrig batted right after "The Babe" in the great

Joe and Seinfeld

Although he did not appear, Joe DiMaggio was part of a *Seinfeld* episode where Kramer swears he saw the Yankee Clipper in a local restaurant having a donut. Of course Jerry and Elaine don't believe him. Catch it on reruns.

Yankees lineup and was in the shadow of Ruth, who was more charismatic than the quiet Gehrig. Nonetheless, Gehrig was as awesome a hitter as anyone. For 14 consecutive years he drove in over 100 runs, topping 170 three times, including an American League record 184 in 1931. He could do it all, getting over 200 hits eight times, 40 home runs five times, and batting over .300 for 13 consecutive years. His 23 grand slam home runs is the all-time high.

Despite all of his amazing accomplishments, Gehrig is best known for two things. He began a streak in 1925 where he played every single game until 1939, or 2,130 consecutive games, a record most people thought would never be broken. Cal Ripken has since topped that incredible record. Unfortunately, the other thing Gehrig is best remembered for is the reason that eight games into the 1939 season he removed himself from the lineup. Gehrig began suffering from an unknown disease, later called Lou Gehrig's disease. He would retire from baseball in May of 1939, and in July he described himself as the luckiest man on earth for the opportunity to have played for the Yankees, and to have been loved by the fans and by his wife. Less than two years later he died at the age of 37. He was elected into the Hall of Fame in 1939.

The Pride of the Yankees, Gehrig's Story

The movie *The Pride of the Yankees* is a marvelous, deeply touching story of this great, courageous man.

Rogers Hornsby Cardinals, Giants, Red Sox, Cubs, Browns

HR	RBI	BA
301	1,584	.358

He was called by those who saw him play and many baseball historians the greatest right-handed hitter in baseball history (Babe Ruth hit from the left side). A dedicated hitter, Hornsby believed that watching movies, drinking coffee, and drinking alcohol would affect his eye at the plate, so he avoided

all of those habits. Starting in 1921 he posted a combined five-year average of .402, which was, in a word, amazing! But Hornsby wasn't just hitting singles on his way to a .358 career average—second all-time to Cobb. He led the league several times in doubles and home runs and posted over 10 triples in a season nine times. Twice Hornsby won the Triple Crown, and twice he won the MVP. He would go on to be a player manager in 1926 and was very successful. The problem was, as good a hitter and manager as Hornsby was, he was very demanding, unfriendly, and considered downright mean. In the late 1920s he was traded from team to team since he wasn't well liked around the clubhouse. Hornsby made the Hall of Fame in 1942.

Reggie Jackson A's, Orioles, Yankees, Angels

HR	RBI	BA
563	1,702	.262

"Mr. October" was Reggie's nickname, because when it was World Series time (in October), he was awesome. A great power hitter from his rookie year in 1967, Jackson would go on to lead the league in home runs four times during his career and end up sixth on the all-time list when he retired. Jackson helped the Oakland A's win three consecutive World Series championships in '72, '73, and '74. He would later join the Yankees and helped lead them to the World Series three times and win two more World Championships. Reggie struck out a lot and wasn't a great defensive star, but when it was an important game, he was at his best. In game six of the 1977 World Series, Jackson had what many consider the single best World Series game of any hitter ever. He hit three tremendous home runs and drove in five runs in the game. Jackson was outspoken and very popular everywhere he went through his entire career. He made the Hall of Fame in 1993.

FUN FACT

Senior Named Hitting Coach

Rogers Hornsby was such a great hitter that at the age of 66 he was hired as the New York Mets' hitting coach. The Mets lost 120 games that year—apparently they didn't listen to him.

FUN FACT

Mr. Switch Hitter

Some hitters bat from the right side and some from the left, but if you can hit from either side of the plate, you're called a switch hitter. The greatest switch hitter of all time was Mickey Mantle. He holds the record for hitting home runs in the same game from both sides of the plate nine different times.

Mickey Mantle Yankees

HR	RBI	BA
536	1,509	.298

When Joe DiMaggio retired in 1951, someone had to fill his shoes, and that was a tall order because he was one of the greatest ever. Sure enough, the Yankees found another super-star, from the town of Spavinaw, Oklahoma: "The Mick," as he was called. Mantle was a star in all aspects of the game. He hit for power, for average, hit in the clutch, and for a while even stole bases. Starting in 1953 Mantle would rattle off nine straight 100+ RBI seasons. He led the league in homers with 52 in 1956 while winning the Triple Crown and MVP. His 54 homers would have led most seasons in 1961, but teammate Roger Maris showed him up by hitting a record 61. Unfortunately, by 1965 injuries would make it difficult for Mantle to play at the same level he had for so many years. Bad knees moved Mantle to first base where he played until 1968. For a span of 12 out of 14 years between 1951 and 1964 the Yankees went to the World Series, largely because of Mantle. His 18 home runs and 40 runs batted in in 65 World Series games are all-time records. Mantle was popular on and off the field, a Yankee legend powering the team to pennant after pennant. He made the Hall of Fame in 1974.

Willie Mays Giants, Mets

HR	RBI	BA
660	1,903	.302

They called him the "Say Hey Kid," and he was truly one of the greatest and most likable players to ever play the game. After his rookie season in 1951, Mays spent two years in the army before returning to the (then New York) Giants and leading them with 41 homers to the World Championship over

the Cleveland Indians. Willie could do it all. He hit for power, leading the league in homers four times, and he also had great speed, leading the league in stolen bases four times. He was also known for incredible defense, with his basket catch, using the glove as a "basket" and catching fly balls at his waist. Perhaps the most famous catch ever made by Mays came in the first game of the 1954 World Series as he grabbed a ball going over his head in the deepest part of center field to help the Giants hold on and win. After many years with the Giants in San Francisco, Mays spent his last couple of years back in New York with the Mets before retiring as the third greatest home run hitter ever. A baseball legend, Mays made the Hall of Fame in 1979.

About Willie Mays

Former Dodger player and manager Gil Hodges talked about how good a defensive player Willie Mays really was. "I can't very well tell my hitters, don't hit it to him. Wherever they hit it, he's always there."

Stan Musial Cardinals

HR	RBI	BA
475	1,951	.331

One of the most feared hitters in the 1940s and '50s was "Stan the Man" Musial. He started as a pitcher in the minor leagues, but an arm injury forced him to switch to playing the outfield. At 23 years old in his second season he won the MVP, which was the first of four he would collect in his 21 incredible seasons. Stan could hit for power, drive in runs, and hit for a high average, leading the league in batting seven times. He worked very hard perfecting his swing, and many young players wanted to learn from him. He spent his entire career with one team, the St. Louis Cardinals, and holds most of the Cardinals' all-time hitting records. Musial was elected to the Hall of Fame in 1969.

Frank Robinson Reds, Orioles, Dodgers, Angels, Indians

HR	RBI	BA
586	1,812	.294

From his Rookie of the Year season in 1956, the Texas-born Robinson made it obvious that he was going to be a star. In the shadow of Mays, Mantle, and Aaron, Robinson very quietly hit over 30 home runs season after season while consistently batting over .300. The Reds, however, felt they could do better, so after the 1965 season they traded Robinson to the Orioles for two pitchers and an outfielder. He responded to being traded by hitting 49 home runs, driving in 122 runs, and batting .316, winning the Triple Crown, the MVP, and leading the Orioles to a sweep over the Dodgers in the World Series—he was also World Series MVP that year. The Reds regretted trading him. He would later top the 500 home run mark while with the Orioles before playing for several other teams near the end of his 21-year career. When he retired he was fourth all-time in home runs. Robinson also became the first African-American manager in 1975, while still playing for the Cleveland Indians. He was elected to the Hall of Fame in 1982.

Jackie Robinson Dodgers, Giants

HR	RBI	BA
137	734	.311

Jackie Robinson broke into the major leagues with the Brooklyn Dodgers in 1947 at the age of 28 after several years in the Negro Leagues. He led the league in stolen bases and won Rookie of the Year honors. But his entry into the majors was far more significant than his stats. Robinson, broke the "color barrier," becoming the first African-American to play in the major leagues, at least since the late 1800s. Making a major statement for his race wasn't new to Robinson, who had been court-martialed out of the United

States Army after he had refused to sit in the back of a bus because of the color of his skin.

The early days of his career were very difficult. Fans, players on other teams, and even many of his own teammates were cruel. Some players even started a petition that said they would not play in the game with him. Somehow, he put up with all the torment and continued proving himself as a first-rate ballplayer.

In 1949 Robinson hit .342, which led the league in batting, and he was named the MVP. In the span of just 10 years he would make a huge breakthrough for the game of baseball. Robinson's legacy continued long after his seven World Series appearances or his induction into the Hall of Fame in 1962. In 1997 at stadiums all over the country, the 50-year anniversary of Robinson's achievement was honored.

WORDS to KNOW

MVP: The MVP is the Most Valuable Player. One player in each league wins the award every year, not only for being a great player but usually for helping their team go to the playoffs or World Series.

Pete Rose Reds, Phillies, Expos

HR	RBI	BA
160	1,314	.303

They called him "Charlie Hustle" because he ran out every play, even when he drew a walk. No one played the game harder than Pete Rose. He was one of the most intense players of his time, in a career that spanned 24 years. He played outfield, third base, second base, and first base before becoming a player manager. Rose had grown up in Cincinnati, so the Reds were his hometown team, and he became their hero as part of the Big Red Machine of the 1970s. Eight times he had more than 200 hits in a season on his way to becoming the all-time leader in base hits. Rose was a tremendous singles and doubles hitter who led the league in batting three times, but more than anything he was a tireless player. By the time he retired he not only had more hits but more at bats and had played in more games than anyone else.

After his career ended it was alleged that Rose had bet on baseball games while manager of the Reds. The evidence

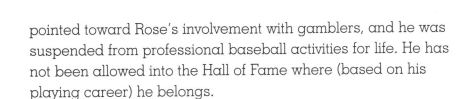

pointed toward Rose's involvement with gamblers, and he was suspended from professional baseball activities for life. He has not been allowed into the Hall of Fame where (based on his playing career) he belongs.

Babe Ruth Red Sox, Yankees, Braves (very briefly)

HR	RBI	BA	W–L	ERA	K
714	2,213	.342	94–46	2.28	488

It's almost impossible to find anyone who hasn't heard of "The Babe." "The Bambino," as he was also nicknamed, George Herman "Babe" Ruth could do it all. He began as a pitcher with the Boston Red Sox (and a good one) before moving to the outfield. He would go on to change the face of baseball. When Ruth led the major leagues with 29 home runs in 1919 it was the first time a player had hit more than 25 in a season. He was traded to the Yankees where he became the greatest home run hitter ever. His 714 home runs stood as the record until Hank Aaron passed that mark in 1974. Had Ruth not been a pitcher for several years, who knows how many he would have hit. He led the league in home runs (or tied for the lead) 12 times. He also batted .342 for his career and is still considered by most baseball historians as the greatest baseball player ever. Ruth led the Yankees to one World Series title after another. A much rumored story says that Ruth once stepped up to the plate and pointed to the bleachers where he was going to hit a home run . . . and he did just that.

Beyond baseball, Ruth was an enormously popular celebrity and was treated like royalty. The Babe enjoyed all the publicity and excitement that surrounded him. It was said that "as he moved, center stage moved with him." Ruth retired in 1935 and was one of the first five players elected to the Hall of Fame in 1939. Yankee stadium is still called The House That Ruth Built.

Home Runs Often

Babe Ruth hit home runs at an incredible rate, averaging 43 per season over a span of 16 years.

Mike Schmidt Phillies

HR	RBI	BA
548	1,595	.267

Mike Schmidt is considered by many to be the best all-around third baseman ever to play the game. He was a truly awesome power hitter, leading the league eight times in home runs. In just 17 years he placed himself in the top 10 all-time in homers, won three MVPs, and helped lead the Phillies to their only World Championship. On the other side of the field, he was a tremendous defensive player. He won the Gold Glove as the best fielding third baseman in the National League nine times. He went about his business very seriously and the fans of the Philadelphia Phillies, as well as other players, respected and admired his talent and his work ethic. Schmidt retired in 1989 and was elected to the Hall of Fame in 1995.

Ozzie Smith Padres, Cardinals

HR	RBI	BA
28	793	.262

How can a player with those kind of career numbers be included in this list of the all-time greats, you may wonder? Just 28 homers in 19 years? Smith represents the other side of the game: defense. They called him the "Wizard of Oz" because no one had ever played shortstop like Ozzie. He could get to groundballs that no one else could reach, often diving in either direction. He would then somehow make the throw to first base for the out. He could also turn the double plays like nobody else, turning more than any player in history. He would dazzle the fans and frustrate the opponents who thought they had a hit until somehow Ozzie turned it into an out. He won a record 13 Gold Gloves and led the league nine times in fielding percentage at shortstop. When Ozzie came up he wasn't much of a hitter, but by the late 1980s he had established himself as a

FUN FACT

Two-Time MVP Winners

The National League has had 10 players who have won the MVP award more than once. By coincidence, there is one at each position so you could field a multi-MVP team (plus a back-up): pitcher Carl Hubbell, catchers Johnny Bench and Roy Campanella, first baseman Stan Musial (he started as an outfielder, shhh), second baseman Joe Morgan, shortstop Ernie Banks, third baseman Mike Schmidt, and outfielders Barry Bonds, Willie Mays, and Dale Murphy. Quite a team, huh?

decent hitter who drew plenty of walks. He could also steal bases, picking up 580 in his 19-year career, or over 30 per year. Smith was a team leader and a fan favorite. He retired in 1996 and is headed to the Hall of Fame in 2001.

Honus Wagner Pirates

HR	RBI	BA
101	1,698	.329

Wagner was one of the first superstars of baseball. He began his career just before the 1900s and was a terrific hitter, base stealer, and a flawless fielder. For 17 years he batted over .300 and led the National League eight times in batting average. He also led the league six times in stolen bases and had over 700 in his career. Playing for the Pirates, Wagner was the shortstop in the first World Series ever played in 1903. In 1909 Wagner asked that the tobacco company printing his baseball card stop making them because he felt that smoking set a bad example for children. Only a few of the cards remained, and today a 1909 Honus Wagner card is the most valuable baseball card you could find, worth more than half a million dollars. Many baseball historians still consider Wagner the greatest all-around shortstop ever, and he was one of a few at that position on the All-Century Team. Wagner was also one of the first five players to go into the Hall of Fame in 1939.

Ted Williams Red Sox

HR	RBI	BA
521	1,839	.344

Ted Williams, known as "The Splendid Splinter" was one of the most remarkable hitters ever. He hit for power, for a high average, and rarely ever struck out. In fact, after his career he wrote a book called *The Science of Hitting*, which is still a terrific book to read for anyone who wants to learn to be a better

hitter. As a rookie in 1939, Williams hit .327 and a couple of years later batted .406. Nearly 50 years later, no one has batted over .400 for a season since. The following year in 1942, he not only led the league in batting average again, but also led with 37 home runs and 137 runs batted in, winning the Triple Crown. Williams' career was interrupted twice, once when he was drafted into the Navy for World War II and the other time when he volunteered to serve in the Korean War. Both times he would return to baseball and have great seasons. Williams finally called it quits at age 42 and was inducted into the Hall of Fame in 1965. Players to this day want his tips on being a better hitter.

The Stars of Today

There are a lot of fabulous ballplayers in the major leagues today. Some are early on in their careers, while others are close to retiring. A few will end up in Cooperstown in the Hall of Fame, while others will simply be remembered for a few magical moments, whether it was a game-winning home run or a fabulous defensive play that won a big game. One of the great things about base-ball is that on any given day anyone can be the big hero. The following, however, are players that have been big heroes on a consistent basis. These are today's stars that will very likely be tomorrow's Hall of Famers.

Premier Pitchers

At a time when home runs are flying out of the ballparks, there are still a few

Activity

Baseball Hangman

Sitting in a restaurant waiting for the waiter to bring your food? If you've got a pen and a paper placemat you can play hangman, but not just any hangman—baseball hangman, featuring major league players current, past, or on your favorite team. Choose your category depending on how well you and your opponent—be it dad, mom, or your brother or sister—know baseball. Put down the first letter and blank spaces for the rest of the names, such as S _ _ _ _ S _ _ _ . Okay, so that's an easy one. Then they have to guess letters as in the game hangman, and you draw a hangman rope and stick figure—see if they get the name before they're hung.

pitchers that shine above and beyond the rest.

Pedro Martinez: His older brother spent years as one of the ace pitchers for the Dodgers, so when Pedro came up (also with the Dodgers) a lot was expected of him. He didn't disappoint. In his first full season he pitched mostly in relief and struck out 119 batters in only 107 innings. He was, however, traded to Montreal, where he became one of the top pitchers in the league. In 1997 he posted a 1.90 ERA and struck out 305 batters, winning the National League Cy Young Award. But it is in Boston where Pedro has taken his pitching to an even higher level. His first two seasons with the Red Sox produced 42 wins, 11 losses, and an American League Cy Young Award. He led the Sox to the post season in 1999 and continues to be the top pitcher in the American League.

Randy Johnson: The slender 6'10" Johnson has become known as "The Big

Play Ball

You must be sure to follow the rules of the game, or you could get sent to the dugout! You must carefully follow the directions below to learn the word that finishes the following popular saying: "Some people say that playing baseball is as American as eating _____."

Yummm! I LOVE this game!

HINT: As you complete each step, write the new combination of letters on the lines to the right.

1. Print the word "BASEBALL." _____

2. Switch the position of the first two letters. _____

3. Move the 5th letter between the 2nd and 3rd letters. _____

4. Switch positions of the 4th and 8th letters. _____

5. Change the 6th letter to a "P." _____

6. Change the last letter to an "E." _____

7. Change both "B"s to "P"s. _____

8. Change the 7th letter to an "I." _____

FUN FACT

No-Hitter and Perfect Game

When a pitcher allows no hits in a game, it's a no-hitter, but when a pitcher allows no hits, no walks, and no base runners at all for an entire game, it's a perfect game. It's very rare!

Unit," as he fires the ball down at hitters who just try to see his fastball, much less hit it. Johnson came up to the big leagues with Montreal in 1988, but it was with the Seattle Mariners that he became the dominating pitcher that he is today. Between 1993 and 1997, Johnson posted a 75–20 win/loss record, had his first 300+ strikeout season, and picked up his first Cy Young Award. In 1998 he was traded to Houston and gave the National League a taste of what American League hitters had to deal with, a blazing fastball and tremendous control. In 1999 he signed with the Arizona Diamondbacks, where he struck out 364 on his way to another Cy Young Award. He also led Arizona to the playoffs in only their second year as a team. Johnson continues to be the top pitcher in the National League.

Greg Maddux: He doesn't have the blazing fastball of a Randy Johnson or put up amazing strikeout totals, but his secret to pitching is, as he puts it, "making your strikes look like balls and your balls look like strikes." Maddux is a very smart pitcher with tremendous control who knows how to get batters out. In 1997, for example, he walked only 14 batters in over 230 innings. He knows how to throw several pitches very well, mixes them up, and can hit the corners of the plate. In 1995 and '96, with the Braves, Greg went a combined 35–8 with a 1.60 ERA, capturing two of his four Cy Young Awards. On his way to becoming one of only a few 300-game winners, Maddux continues to be a super pitcher.

Roger Clemens: In 1986, a young Clemens led the Red Sox to the World Series, posting a 24–4 record while winning his first of an amazing five Cy Young Awards. Clemens holds the record for most strikeouts in a game (20), which he accomplished twice. "The Rocket," as he was nicknamed, now has over 3,500 strike-outs and is heading toward 300 wins and the Hall of Fame as his career winds down. Along with Greg Maddux, Clemens was one

of two active pitchers named to the All-Century Team of the 100 all-time greatest players of the twentieth century by Major League Baseball.

While Pedro, The Big Unit, and Greg Maddux are still among the cream of the crop, **Tom Glavine** is another star of the Braves pitching staff and has been for over a decade, winning 20 or more games four times and two Cy Young Awards. Dodgers ace **Kevin Brown**, **Curt Schilling** of the Phillies, and the Orioles' **Mike Mussina** have been among the top starters in recent years, while **Mariano Rivera** (Yankees), **Trevor Hoffman** (Padres), and **John Wetteland** (Rangers) have been among the most consistent closers, piling up saves year in and year out.

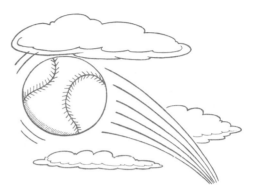

Top Hitters

Each year it seems that there are more and more hitters belting 20 or 30 home runs per season as hitters get bigger and stronger. There are also a lot of good hitters hitting for a high average and many who can steal a fair number of bases. Below are a few of the game's superstar hitters.

Barry Bonds: Barry's dad, Bobby, was a terrific player for the Giants and Yankees, but Barry has surpassed even dad's great ability. Barry can do it all. He hits for power, a high average, steals bases, and plays great defense. The young Bonds came up with the Pirates in 1986. By the 1990s he had turned from a good player into a superstar. He was the most feared hitter in baseball in the early 1990s, winning the MVP in 1990, 1992, and 1993. Still going strong in the late '90s, he is the only player in major league history to hit over 400 home runs and steal over 400 bases and will soon top 500 in both categories.

Ken Griffey Jr.: They call him "Junior," and like Bonds, his dad was a major league ballplayer. In fact, when he joined the

Picture This #4

This picture "spells" a well known baseball play.

Who's Who?

Some baseball nicknames are easy to guess. For example, almost all players who have had the last name "Rhodes" have gotten the nickname "Dusty." See how many of the famous nicknames on the left you can match with the real names on the right. Put the number of the correct nickname on the line in front of each real name.

1. The Big Train	___ Cy Young
2. Tom Terrific	___ Jimmy Foxx
3. Cyclone	___ Joe DiMaggio
4. Yankee Clipper	___ Mark McGwire
5. Double XX	___ Mickey Mantle
6. Mr. October	___ Ozzie Smith
7. The Mick	___ Pete Rose
8. Say Hey Kid	___ Randy Johnson
9. Stan The Man	___ Reggie Jackson
10. Charlie Hustle	___ Roger Clemens
11. Wizard of Oz	___ Sammy Sosa
12. The Big Unit	___ Stan Musial
13. The Rocket	___ Tom Seaver
14. Big Mac	___ Walter Johnson
15. Slammin' Sammy	___ Willie Mays

majors in 1989 he played on the Seattle Mariners with his dad—the only time that's ever happened. Griffey, who genuinely loves to play the game, is one of the greatest center fielders ever, making many amazing catches and winning the Gold Glove for defense every year. He is a major home run threat as well and is often compared to the great Willie Mays. Griffey hit 56 home runs in 1997 and again in 1998 with over 140 RBIs each year. At just over 30 years of age, Griffey has already topped 400 home runs and is on his way to 500, and probably plenty more in a sensational career.

Juan Gonzalez: Playing for Texas and Detroit, Juan does not get all the attention of ballplayers in New York, Chicago, or Los Angeles. However, he has quietly put together a Hall of Fame career. The Puerto Rican native, known as "Juan Gone" for his "out of sight" home runs, had hit over 40 home runs five times and won the MVP award before turning 30. Gonzalez is on his way to 500 or 600 home runs and will probably win another MVP award or two before he retires.

Tony Gwynn: No, he's not a big power hitter like McGwire, Bonds, or Sosa, but since he came up to the big leagues, Gwynn has been the best hitter in baseball and one of the best of all time. His career .338 average is up there with the greats of the early 1900s, and in 1994 he came within 6 points of batting .400, something which hasn't been done since 1941. Gwynn has led the league in batting seven times, hitting over .360 four times. He knows how to hit any pitch for a single or double and hardly ever strikes out, which helps explain why he has over 3,000 career hits. In his younger years he was also a great base stealer and tremendous defensive player. Now, nearing the end of his career, Gwynn is a shoo-in for the Hall of Fame.

Mark McGwire: It began in 1987 when he joined slugger Jose Canseco on the Oakland A's. Together they became known as the "Bash Brothers," clobbering monster home runs.

Big Mac hit 49 in his first year, setting a rookie record and winning Rookie of the Year honors. In 1989, along with Canseco, the power pair led the A's to the World Championship. The early '90s saw a series of injuries slow things down for Mark. In 1996, however, he was back in form, hitting 52 homers for the A's. the following year they traded him midseason to the Cardinals. That year he hit 58 homers. That set the stage for the incredible season of 1998 when Mark went from a star to an American hero. Everyone was rooting for McGwire, even Sammy Sosa, who battled with him for the home run record. By the time the 1998 season was over, McGwire had shattered the home run record of 61 by hitting an amazing 70 home runs! Now he is headed toward 600 career homers (only three players have hit more than 600) if his sore back and bad knee lets him keep on playing. He's great fun to watch, so much so that fans show up early to see him club balls out of the stadium in batting practice.

Big Unit

The tallest pitcher in baseball history is still playing today, and he is "The Big Unit," Randy Johnson, who stands 6'10" tall.

Mike Piazza: Move over Johnny Bench, here comes Piazza. Through eight major league seasons Piazza, who still needs a nickname, has put up incredible numbers, including a career .332 batting average and nearly 300 homers. Piazza was not expected to do the things he has done. In fact, over 200 players were selected ahead of him in the amateur draft. His godfather, Tommy Lasorda (former Dodgers manager) drafted Mike as a favor to his pal, Mike's dad. Mike repaid the favor by winning Rookie of the Year honors in 1993 and never stopped hitting. Barring injury,

What would be a good baseball nickname for you? It can have something to do with your name, the way you look, or the way you play the game. Write your nickname on the line below.

_____

Piazza is en route to being remembered as the greatest offensive catcher in baseball history.

Cal Ripken Jr.: Cal won Rookie of the Year in 1982, MVP in 1983 and again in 1991, and proceeded to establish himself as one of the top players in modern baseball. One thing that could be said for Ripken was that he always came to play, and play hard, day in and day out. Then in late 1995, Cal went from a star to a legend as he broke a record that most thought could never be topped. Cal played in his 2,131st consecutive game, breaking the iron-horse record set by the late great Lou Gehrig. Cal played another 501 more consecutive games before taking himself out of the lineup in September of 1998. He will surely go to the Hall of Fame when his career ends. He has over 3,000 hits, 400 home runs, and 1,700 RBIs. He's also one of the best-liked and most respected individuals in the game of baseball.

Sammy Sosa: Slammin' Sammy Sosa, from the small town of San Pedro de Macoris in the Dominican Republic, grew up dreaming of being a ballplayer. His family and friends were poor, so a baseball game consisted of Sammy and the local boys using rolled up socks for a ball and milk cartons for gloves. Sammy was discovered and signed at age 16, and by 21 he was in the big leagues. After a few so-so seasons, Sammy's career took off as a member of the Cubs. In 1998 he made front page news as he battled with Mark McGwire for the all-time home run record. Sammy finished the season with 66 home runs and the following year with 63. Both totals were more than anyone had ever hit in the long history of the game, except for McGwire, who hit 70 and 65. Sosa did one better than McGwire, though, by winning the 1998 MVP as he led the Cubs to the playoffs. Whether he ever wins a

Who Said Pitchers Can't Hit?

In 1942, Jim Tobin hit three home runs in one game. In the 1960s, Tony Clonginger hit two grand slams. No other pitchers have ever equalled these records.

home run title or not, Sammy will always be remembered as one of the greats of baseball, both on and off the field.

Frank Thomas and **Albert Belle:** Teammates for two years, 1997 and 1998 on the White Sox, these two ballplayers emerged as dominant hitters in 1991 and have both put up 30 and 40 home runs nearly every year since with big 100+ seasons and .300 averages. Thomas, known as "The Big Hurt," won the MVP in 1993 and posted batting averages of .353, .349, and .347 in the mid-'90s, while Belle, who sometimes gets himself in trouble with the media, his teammates, and the fans, has let his bat do his talking, batting .357 in 1994 and hitting 50 homers in 1995. Both remain two of the most feared sluggers in the game today.

Other Stars of Today

There are many other great hitters in baseball today. Three marvelous young shortstops, Derek Jeter, Nomar Garciapara, and Alex Rodriguez are lighting up the American League. Jeter and Garciapara battled for the 1999 batting crown with Nomar winning the honors, .357 to .349. Meanwhile, Rodriguez belted 42 homers in both 1998 and 1999, proving once again that shortstops can hit the long ball, too. Veteran National League shortstop Barry Larkin has been an All-Star year after year, as a .300 hitter, base stealer, and team leader for the Reds. Third baseman Chipper Jones followed up four excellent seasons with an MVP year in 1999 when he emerged as a superstar with 45 home runs while leading the Braves to the World Series.

On the other side of the infield, second basemen Roberto Alomar and Craig Biggio have combined speed with power, plus .300+ batting averages and fine defensive play to be the

First MVP Players

The first ever MVP winners were Lefty Grove in the American League, and pitcher and second baseman Frankie Frisch in the National League.

FUN FACT

A Coincidence

Odd as it may seem, in *The Baseball Encyclopedia*, which has over 1,000 pages of players listed, the first player in the book (alphabetically) is also the first player in home runs, Hank Aaron.

44!

In 1963 the National League home run leaders were number 44 on the Giants, Willie McCovey, and number 44 on the Braves, Hank Aaron. Guess how many they each hit? 44!

tops at their positions over the past decade. Power-hitting Jeff Kent and Edgardo Alfonso, who hits for a high average, are also among the best second basemen in the game today. Plenty of solid-hitting first baseman lead their teams in power and average. Jeff Bagwell of the Astros hits for power and steals bases. Carlos Delgado of Toronto and Todd Helton of the Rockies are emerging as the new superstars at the position.

While Piazza is rewriting the numbers offensively for catchers, Ivan "Pudge" Rodriguez is an outstanding defensive catcher who in 1999 went from a good hitter to a great hitter, with 35 homers and 113 RBIs, plus a .332 average. Look out Mike—Pudge even stole 25 bases!

Outfielders have traditionally, along with first basemen, been the best hitters. Manny Ramirez of the Indians had a combined RBI total in 1998 and 1999 of 310! Larry Walker, Gary Sheffield, Shawn Green, Bernie Williams, Vladimir Guerrero, and young Andruw Jones are all among the many star outfielders in the major leagues today. One of the veteran outfielders, now wrapping up his long career, is known as the greatest lead-off hitter in baseball history. Rickey Henderson set the major league record by stealing 130 bases in 1982, topping the record set by Lou Brock of 118. Henderson has gone on in his career of over 20 years to steal over 1,300 bases, by far the most ever. Rickey will be in the Hall of Fame in a few years.

FUN FACT

Hall of Fame Quotes

They called him Mr. Cub, Ernie Banks. The cheerful former shortstop of the Cubs was a two-time MVP who loved to play so much that he became known for saying, "It's a great day for a ballgame. Let's play two."

One of baseball's best-known quotes comes from former Yankee catcher Yogi Berra, who said, "It ain't over 'til it's over." If you've ever seen a team make a great comeback, you'll realize that Yogi was right!

A true character of the game, Hall of Fame pitcher Dizzy Dean was always known for bragging and clowning around. He was quoted as saying "It ain't braggin' if you can back it up."

In 1936, the baseball community decided that a place to honor the greatest players ever was needed. So, the idea for the Hall of Fame was born. Then in June of 1939, the National Baseball Hall of Fame and Museum was opened in Cooperstown, New York.

It is a great place to visit for three or four days . . . a place where you'll find bats and gloves used by the greatest players, balls that were hit for historic home runs, and plenty of other neat baseball stuff. A trip to the Hall of Fame is a must for any baseball fan. The Hall includes plaques honoring the 244 members, which include 183 great players along with managers and other people closely associated with the game. There are even a few umpires included. It is the greatest honor for anyone involved with baseball to end up in the Hall of Fame and the dream of every fan to drop by for a visit.

Popular Hall of Fame Exhibits

The three-floor Hall of Fame Museum has many exhibits in different rooms that honor different parts of the game.

"The Great American Home Run Chase" pays tribute to the always exciting chase to see if anyone would break the record for most home runs in a season. Featured are balls, bats, and other items from the only four players ever to hit more than 60 homers in one season: Babe Ruth, Roger Maris, Mark McGwire, and Sammy Sosa.

The "Today's Stars" exhibit has all sorts of information about the current stars of the game.

"Baseball Around the World" gives fans a look at how baseball is played in other countries such as Japan, where baseball has

been played for decades, and Cuba where the game is very popular.

A "No-Hitters" exhibit honors the pitchers who have pitched no-hit games throughout baseball history. Nolan Ryan, who pitched an incredible seven no-hitters, is prominently featured.

"The World Series Room" has all sorts of displays and memorabilia from what is called "The Fall Classic," the World Series, where the best of the American League and the best of the National League meet every year to determine baseball's champion.

"Hail to the Champs" honors the most recent World Series winners. This is particularly a place to visit if your favorite team took home the honors.

"The Evolution of Equipment" is really cool, as it shows how bats, balls, gloves, catcher's masks, and uniforms have changed over the many years of the great game.

"Pride and Passion" is an exhibit honoring the African-American experience in baseball, including the Negro Leagues and memorabilia from the great players, including Jackie Robinson.

"Ballparks" has actual seats, dugout benches, and even turnstiles from many of the great ballparks that have been torn down and replaced by newer stadiums over the years.

There is so much to see, including films and even an actual ballfield where two major league teams square off every summer in a special exhibition game. The Hall of Fame also has special programs that include "sandlot stories" about the game, movies, and book signings by some of the many authors who write about the game, which often include former players,

FUN FACT

An Honor

Making the Hall of Fame is a tremendous honor that only a few of the many baseball players ever receive. To make the Hall of Fame a player must be retired from baseball for five years.

Players are voted in by baseball writers. Generally only two players make the Hall of Fame every year. There is also a special committee that votes in veterans of the game, which include real old-timers from the 1800s, players from the Negro Leagues, managers, baseball executives, broadcasters, or others associated with the game in some manner.

Brothers

Twenty-five Hall of Famers had a brother who played in the major leagues, but none of them were twins.

What about Third Base?

There have been many great third basemen in baseball history, but only eleven have made the Hall of Fame, the fewest of any position.

Not the Yankees

Do you know which team has the most players in the Hall of Fame? It's the Giants, not the Yankees, with 23.

managers, and popular broadcasters. There's even a daily scavenger hunt for kids to take part in during the summer months. You may have to move through the Hall of Fame slowly because (a) it's crowded, and (b) there's so much to check out!

A Little History of the Hall

The idea for the Hall of Fame began in Cooperstown in the 1930s. Cooperstown was where Abner Doubleday, who many feel invented the game, had lived, so it seemed to be the ideal place to build such a museum to honor the game. In 1936, as baseball approached it's one hundredth anniversary, plans were made to honor the greatest players of the game. That year, the first five players, Ty Cobb, Babe Ruth, Honus Wagner, Christy Mathewson, and Walter Johnson were voted in as the first players to make the Hall of Fame. By 1939, the actual building was completed. There was a big ceremony that summer, and the Hall of Fame was officially opened, displaying all sorts of stuff from the game to that point. It was a small museum at first, but thousands of people flocked to tiny Cooperstown to visit. Over the years the Hall has grown, with new wings added on to accommodate all of the new exhibits plus a gallery, a library, and more. Today, between 300,000 and 400,000 visit the baseball shrine annually. That's quite a lot of visitors for a town that has only 2,300 people.

The Hall of Fame Players

Catchers

Johnny Bench
Yogi Berra
Roger Bresnahan
Roy Campanella
Mickey Cochrane
Bill Dickey
Buck Ewing
Rick Ferrell
Carlton Fisk
Josh Gibson (Negro Leagues)
Gabby Hartnett
Ernie Lombardi
Ray Schalk

First Basemen

Cap Anson
Jake Beckley
Jim Bottomley
Dan Brouthers
Orlando Cepeda
Frank Chance
Oscar Charleston (Negro Leagues)
Roger Connor
Jimmie Foxx
Lou Gehrig
Hank Greenberg
George Kelly
Harmon Killebrew
Buck Leonard
Willie McCovey
Johnny Mize
Tony Pérez
George Sisler
Bill Terry

Second Basemen

Rod Carew
Eddie Collins
Bobby Doerr
Johnny Evers
Nellie Fox
Frankie Frisch
Charlie Gehringer
Billy Herman
Rogers Hornsby
Nap Lajoie
Tony Lazzeri
Bid McPhee
Joe Morgan
Jackie Robinson
Red Schoendienst

Shortstops

Luis Aparicio
Luke Appling
Dave Bancroft
Ernie Banks
Lou Boudreau
Joe Cronin
George Davis
Travis Jackson
Hugh Jennings
Pop Lloyd
Rabbit Maranville
Pee Wee Reese
Phil Rizzuto
Joe Sewell
Joe Tinker
Arky Vaughn
Honus Wagner
Bobby Wallace
John Ward
Willie Wells
Robin Yount

Third Basemen

Frank "Home Run" Baker
George Brett
Jimmy Collins
Ray Dandridge
Judy Johnson (Negro Leagues)
George Kell
Fred Lindstrom
Eddie Mathews
Brooks Robinson
Mike Schmidt
Pie Traynor

Outfielders

Hank Aaron
Richie Ashburn
Earl Averill
James "Cool Papa" Bell
    (Negro Leagues)
Lou Brock
Jesse Burkett
Max Carey
Fred Clarke
Roberto Clemente
Ty Cobb
Earle Combs
Sam Crawford
Kiki Cuyler
Ed Delahanty
Joe DiMaggio
Larry Doby
Hugh Duffy
Elmer Flick
Goose Goslin
Chick Hafey
Billy Hamilton
Harry Heilmann
Harry Hooper
Monte Irvin

Reggie Jackson
Al Kaline
Willie Keeler
Joe Kelley
King Kelly
Ralph Kiner
Chuck Klein
Mickey Mantle
Heinie Manush
Willie Mays
Tommy McCarthy
Joe Medwick
Stan Musial
Jim O'Rourke
Mel Ott
Sam Rice
Frank Robinson
Edd Roush
George Herman "Babe" Ruth
Al Simmons
Enos Slaughter
Duke Snider
Tris Speaker
Willie Stargell
Turkey Stearnes
Sam Thompson
Lloyd Waner
Paul Waner
Zack Wheat
Billy Williams
Ted Williams
Hack Wilson
Carl Yastrzemski
Ross Youngs

Pitchers

Pete Alexander
Chief Bender
Mordecai Brown
Jim Bunning
Steve Carlton
Jack Chesbro
John Clarkson
Stan Coveleski
Leon Day (Also 2B and OF)
Dizzy Dean
Martin Dihigo (Negro Leagues)
Don Drysdale
Red Faber
Bob Feller
Rollie Fingers
Whitey Ford
Bill Foster
Pud Galvin
Bob Gibson
Lefty Gómez
Burleigh Grimes
Lefty Grove
Jesse Haines
Waite Hoyt
Carl Hubbell
Jim "Catfish" Hunter
Fergie Jenkins
Walter Johnson
Addie Joss
Tim Keefe
Sandy Koufax
Bob Lemon
Ted Lyons
Juan Marichal
Rube Marquard
Christy Mathewson

Joe McGinnity
Hal Newhouser
Kid Nichols
Phil Niekro
Satchel Paige (Negro Leagues)
Jim Palmer
Herb Pennock
Gaylord Perry
Eddie Plank
Charley Radbourn
Eppa Rixey
Robin Roberts
Bullet Rogan
Red Ruffing
Amos Rusie
Nolan Ryan
Tom Seaver
Warren Spahn
Don Sutton
Dazzy Vance
Rube Waddell
Ed Walsh
Mickey Welch
Hoyt Wilhelm
Joe Williams
Vic Willis
Early Wynn
Cy Young

It's safe to say these are the greatest players in base-ball history—plus Pete Rose and Joe Jackson, two players banned from baseball for alleged gambling.

76

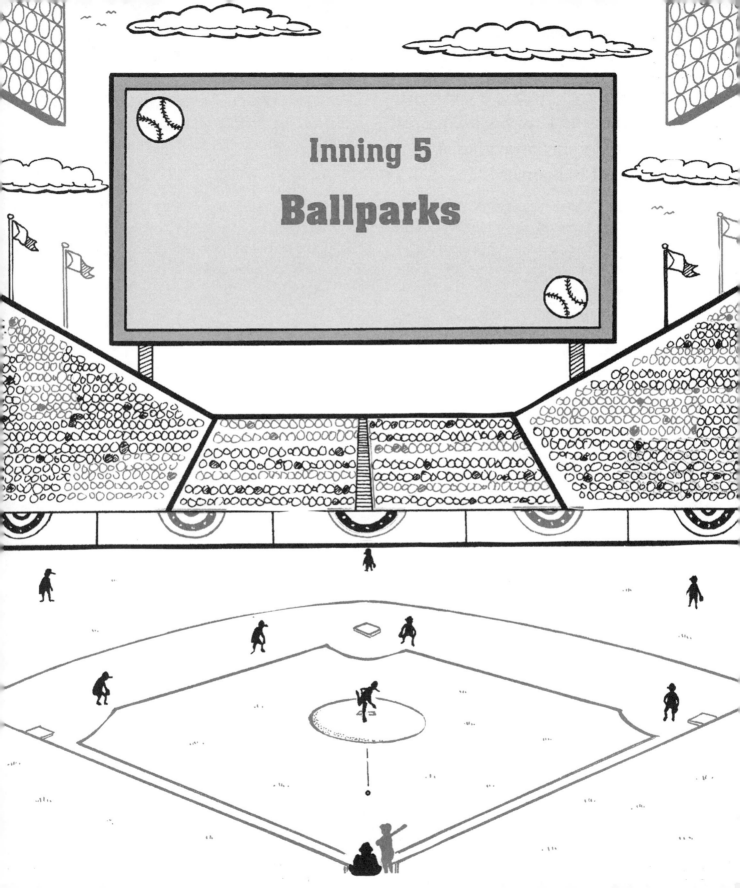

You can't play baseball if you don't have a place to play. So, ballparks, also known today as stadiums, are the home of ballgames.

In baseball, like in most sports, some things need to be the same on every field. For example, the bases are always 90 feet apart and the pitchers mound is always 60½ feet away from home plate. Other parts of the ballparks can be different. The distance from home plate to the outfield fences may be different from one ball park to another. Some ballparks are indoors and others are outdoors. Some even have what are called retractable roofs, which means the roof can be pulled back from the stadium. There are ballparks that don't have real grass but instead have artificial grass called "turf."

Seventh Inning Stretch

This fan has decided to stretch her legs and go get a hot dog.
Can you help her find the correct path back to her seat?

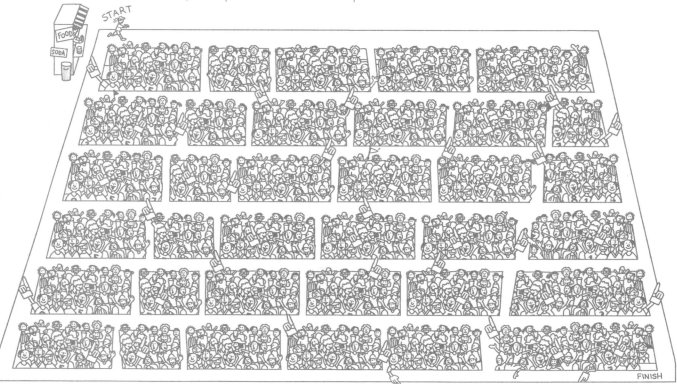

Neat New Ballparks

Arizona Diamondbacks

Bank One Ballpark

Opened: 1998

Capacity: 48,569

The lowdown: The stadium is right smack in the city of Phoenix.

Features: A retractable roof, natural grass, and a swimming pool behind the outfield fence.

Houston Astros

Enron Field

Opened: 2000

Capacity: 42,000

Lowdown: The Astros left the pitcher-friendly Astrodome for the pitcher-unfriendly new ballpark and had a very hard time adjusting in their first year.

Features: A retractable roof that can slide on and off of the ballpark in 20 minutes, a kids' play area, a modern sound system, and retail stores.

San Francisco Giants

Pacific Bell Park

Opened: 2000

Capacity 40,800

Lowdown: The new ballpark sits right by the San Francisco Bay.

Features: Only ballpark where a long home run can result in a splashing sound as the

Le Expos

The city of Montreal is an English- and French-speaking city. The ballpark, Olympic Stadium, where the Expos play, is the only stadium that uses two languages on the scoreboard, on signs, and for announcements.

ball goes into the bay. There's also a giant baseball glove over the outfield wall, a giant soda bottle, stores, and a fence along the waterfront where people watch the game for free.

Detroit Tigers

Comerica Park

Opened: 2000

Capacity: Approximately 42,000

Lowdown: After nearly 40 years in Tiger Stadium, the Tigers moved into a brand new ballpark in 2000.

Features: Computers available to look up statistics and a small theater in which fans can watch a film about Tiger stars like Ty Cobb, Hank Greenberg, and Al Kaline.

Seattle Mariners

Safeco Field
Opened 1999
Capacity: 46,621
Lowdown: New ballpark built like Camden Yards to have an old-fashioned feel, except for the roof.
Features: Retractable roof, a baseball museum, kids' play space, a team store, and picnic areas. The stadium will host the 2001 All-Star Game.

Classic Old Ballparks

Chicago Cubs

Wrigley Field
Opened: 1914
Capacity: 38,902
The Lowdown: Wrigley Field is more than a ballpark; it's a landmark in Chicago. The Cubs moved in back in 1926.
Features: Ivy-covered outfield walls, an old hand-operated scoreboard, a very cozy little ballpark that has charm and character.

Boston Red Sox

Fenway Park
Opened: 1912
Capacity: 34,218
Lowdown: The oldest and smallest ballpark in the major leagues sits right in the heart of Boston.

Features: The Green Monster, the name given to the 37-foot-high green wall that is the left field fence. Inside the Monster is a hand-operated scoreboard, and high atop is a 23-foot netting that catches home runs before they fly onto the streets that surround the park. A great old-fashioned ballpark.

New York Yankees

Yankee Stadium
Opened: 1923
Capacity: 67,000
Lowdown: They call it "The House That Ruth Built" in honor of the Babe.
Features: Monuments honoring Yankee greats sit in Monument Park, which is a mini Hall of Fame of sorts. There are even stadium tours of this great classic old ballpark, which is a must-see site for visitors to the city.

What's the Name Today?

The San Diego Padres have played in the same stadium since 1969, but you'd never know it.

The ballpark, now called Qualcomm Stadium, has had three different names and the owners have changed the number of seats 15 times in 31 years.

Activity

Collecting Stadium Postcards

Okay, so it's not likely that you are going to get to visit all 30 major league cities any time soon. BUT, you can collect postcards of all the stadiums. Every city has stadium postcards. All you have to do is make a list of who you know in different cities around the country or who you know who will be visiting another city in the country and ask them to pick up a postcard of the ballpark for you. You can pay them back with your allowance or maybe they'd like a postcard from your hometown. And, to make it interesting, find a friend who wants to do it, too, then set a date of one year away and see who was able to track down the most stadiums by that date. You'd be surprised how many people you know, such as aunts, uncles, neighbors, and friends, are traveling to another city or have a friend or relative living in a city with a major league ballclub. It's fun trying to track them down, and they're a nice collection to start. When you get older you'll be able to pick up more yourself as you travel.

On Turf

Phillies infielder Dick Allen once summed up his feelings about astroturf in ballparks, "If a cow can't eat it, I don't want to play on it," said Allen.

High in the Sky Ballpark

Colorado Rockies

Coors Field

Opened: 1995

Capacity: 50,381

Lowdown: The ballpark sits over 5,000 feet above sea level where the air is thinner, which means that when the ball is hit it travels farther than at any other stadium. Hitters love Coors, while pitchers hate it.

Features: An old-fashioned clock tower at the entrance and a hand-operated scoreboard in right field. Also a modern heating system under the field that will help melt the snow—and Denver gets a lot of snow.

New Park, Old Look

Baltimore Orioles

Oriole Park at Camden Yards

Opened: 1992

Capacity: 48,262

Lowdown: A new ballpark with an old-time flavor. People come from all over the east coast to check out the stadium and surrounding waterfront area.

Features: An old-fashioned brick look on the outside, a giant building called the Warehouse overlooking the stadium and giving it an the old time feeling. Inside the Warehouse is a gift shop and cafeteria.

WORDS to KNOW

Foul Pole: At every stadium you will see two poles in the outfield at the end of the foul lines. If the ball goes on one side of the pole it's a home run and on the other side it's a foul ball.

Commentators: The commentators are the broadcasters or announcers who are at the ballpark describing what is going on in the game for either television or radio.

FUN FACT

Babe Number Two

The Babe is not only second on the most home runs ever hit, but he has the second most World Series home runs ever hit at 15. Yes, it's another Yankee ahead of him, Mickey Mantle at 18.

The Saver

Yankee relief pitcher John Wetteland set a World Series record in 1996 by being the first pitcher ever to save all four wins for his team in the World Series.

Playing Long Ball

The 1956 Series is not only remembered for Don Larsen's perfect game, but it was also the Series in which the Yankees set a record for the most homers by a team in one series—they hit twelve, including three apiece by Mickey Mantle and Yogi Berra.

"The Fall Classic," as it is often called, is the peak of the baseball season, where the best in the American League and the best in the National League square off for the championship of Major League Baseball. The World Series began in 1903 and has grown in excitement ever since. The World Series is the best of seven games, or the first team to win four games. In 1903, and again in 1918 through 1920, the series became the best of nine, but that was changed back to the standard best of seven that we know today.

Lots of Series Games

Catcher Yogi Berra of the Yankees played in the most World Series games ever, 75.

For many years the American and National League teams never met until the World Series, which followed the season immediately. There were no playoffs, just eight teams in each league, the best of which would win the pennant for their league, and the two teams would go right to the series. In 1969, when the leagues went to 12 teams each, they were divided into two groups, or two divisions, of six each, East and West. This began the playoffs that preceded the Series. Now there are 30 major league teams and three divisions in each league (East, Central, and West) plus two rounds of playoffs. But, no matter how they get there, the pennant-winning teams in each league meet in the World Series.

The Yankees, by far, have appeared in the most Fall Classics and won more than any other team. Between 1927 and 1964 the Yankees were almost always in the Series. At the end of the twentieth century, the Yankees put their stamp on the World Series by winning three of the last four titles of the century, giving them 27 World Series titles overall.

The pressure is on when it gets down to World Series time. Players are in the spotlight, with millions of people watching all over the world. Some players rise to the occasion, while others struggle. There have been many great World Series featuring many different heroes.

Not a Yankee

Cardinals pitcher Bob Gibson won seven World Series games in only three trips to the Series. In one game he struck out 17 batters!

World Series Highlights

1903: On September 16 the first World Series ever began between the Pittsburgh Pirates and the Boston Pilgrims. The Pirates won the Series five games to three. Cy Young won two games.

1905: The New York Giants beat the Philadelphia A's four games to one. All five games were shutouts. Christy Mathewson pitched an incredible three complete game shutouts and walked only one batter for the most amazing pitching performance in World Series history.

1918: Babe Ruth won two games as a pitcher and the Red Sox won their third World Series in four years, beating the Cubs four

games to two. They have never won a Series since.

1919: The White Sox became the Black Sox after they lost the Series to the Reds, five games to three, and were accused of losing the Series on purpose because they were paid money by gamblers. Eight White Sox were banned from baseball for life.

1921: The Giants beat the Yankees five games to three in the first ever all–New York "Subway" Series.

1936: The Yankees scored 18 runs in Game 2 and 13 runs in Game 6 en route to a 4–2 Series win over their cross-the-river rivals, the Giants. It was the Yankees' first post-Ruth

Yikes

Pitcher George Frazier holds a Yankee World Series record that he's not very proud of. In 1981 he lost three of the four games the Yankees would lose to the Dodgers in the series. Poor George.

World Series and featured Lou Gehrig and Joe DiMaggio together for the first time in post season.

1944: The first all–St. Louis World Series had the Browns (who became the Orioles) against the Cardinals. A total of only 28 runs were scored by the two teams in a six-game Series won by the Cardinals 4–2.

1954: In a 2–2 opening game between the Giants and the Indians, Willie Mays made what may be baseball's most famous catch running to the deepest part of centerfield and grabbing the ball with his back to home plate to keep the score tied. The Giants won the Series 4–0.

1955: After losing five times to the Yankees in the World Series, the Brooklyn Dodgers would finally defeat the Yankees four games to three to win their only World Championship. Duke Snider hit four homers and Johnny Podres pitched two complete game victories, including a Game 7 shutout.

1956: Don Larsen pitched the only ever World Series perfect game for the Yankees, who beat the Dodgers once again, this time in seven games, 4–3.

1960: Bill Mazeroski hit one of the most famous home runs ever in the bottom of the ninth inning of the seventh game to lead the Pirates to a victory over the Yankees.

1966: An amazing Orioles pitching staff shut the Dodgers out three consecutive times, including two 1–0 game, to complete a four-game sweep. The Dodgers had only 2 runs on 17 hits in four games.

1969: The team known as the worst in baseball for their first seven years, the Mets, came from nowhere to win 100 games and beat the favored Orioles 4–1 in the Series. Game 3 featured two amazing diving catches by Mets outfielder Tommie Agee.

1975: One of the most famous World Series home runs came in the bottom of the twelfth inning of Game 6 by Red Sox Hall of Fame catcher Carlton Fisk to force a seventh game. The Reds would win that seventh game and the Series, 4–3. Five games were decided by one run in this very close Series.

1977: Reggie Jackson hit three consecutive home runs in the sixth game to lead the Yankees to a 4–2 Series win over the LA Dodgers. Jackson hit five home runs and batted .450 in the Series.

1980: Tug McGraw struck out batters with the bases loaded in Games 5 and 6 to secure two wins for the Phillies, who won their first ever World Series title. Hall of Famer Steve Carlton and Mike Schmidt were Phillie heroes.

1986: Down to their final out in Game 6, the Mets rallied in the tenth inning to beat the Red Sox on a ground ball through first baseman Bill Buckner's legs to win a dramatic game six and proceed to win the Series in seven games.

1988: An injured Kirk Gibson pinch hit a dramatic two-run homer to win the first game of the Series for the Dodgers over the favored Oakland A's. The homer got the Dodgers off to a 4–1 Series win.

1993: For only the second time in World Series history, the Series ended on a game-winning home run. The famous homer came off the bat of Toronto Blue Jay's slugger Joe Carter who gave the Jays an 8–6 win in the sixth and final game of the Series.

1999: The Yankees made it look easy as they won their third title in four years and secured their place as team of the decade, beating the Braves 4–0. It was the fourth time in seven years the Braves lost the World Series.

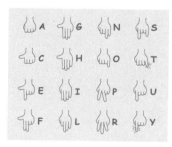

Secret Signals

Use the decoder to figure out what message the catcher signaled to the pitcher when the crab came up to bat.

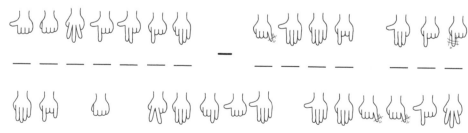

Lucky Numbers

Baseball is a game full of numbers. There's the RBI and ERA numbers, the numbers on the scoreboard, and, of course, the lucky number on the shirt of your favorite player!

In this tricky little puzzle, you must figure out what lucky combination of numbers to use so that each column (up and down) or row (across) adds up to the totals shown in the white numbers. The white arrows show you in which direction you will be adding. Lucky you—four numbers are in place to get you started!

Here are the rules:
- You are only adding the numbers in any set of white boxes that are touching each other.
- Use only the numbers 1 through 9. Each number can only be used once in each set.
- Remember that each number has to be correct both across and down!

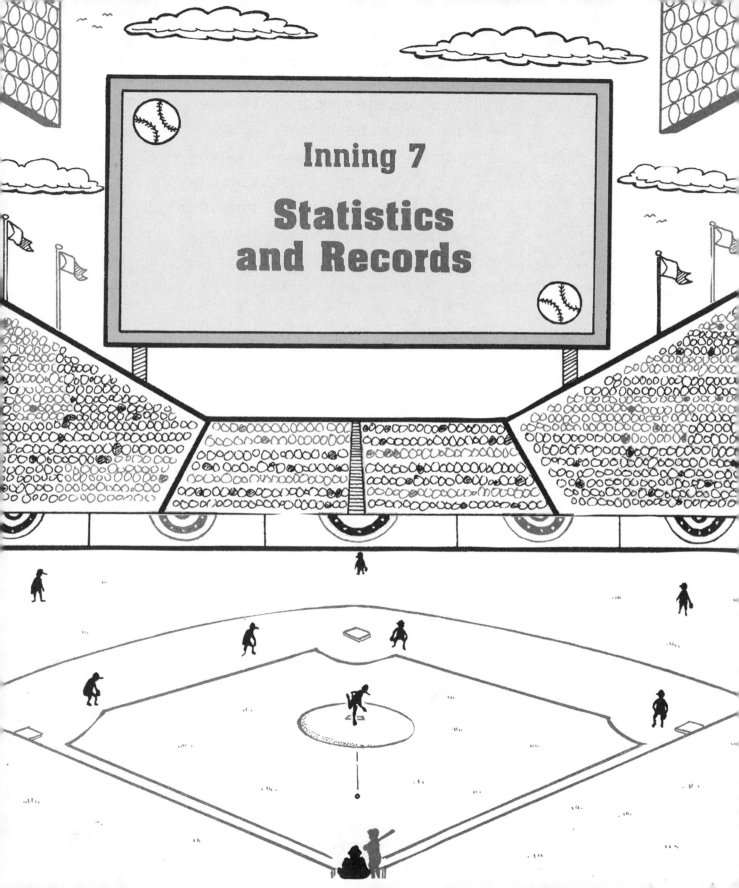

Inning 7

Statistics and Records

Stats, Inc.

Every year a company called Stats, Inc. puts out books filled with baseball stats.

Statistics are very much a part of baseball—more than in any other sport. Since the beginning of the sport, fans have wanted to know who has the most hits, who made the error, who got the win, and so on. Home run totals, batting averages, wins, strikeouts—they are all very much a part of baseball's popularity.

Sometimes when a player is on the verge of breaking a record, like when Cal Ripken Jr. played in his 2,131st game, or when Hank Aaron hit home run number 715, the individual achievements of the players get more attention than the ballgame. That's part of what makes baseball so cool. Your team may not be doing well, like the Cardinals in 1998, but you'll want to watch them to see a great slugger like McGwire pile up home runs on his way to a record.

Players' individual statistics, or "stats," are followed closely, not only by fans but by sportswriters, team management, and everyone associated with baseball. There are actually thousands of statistics that are recorded in baseball, from how long it took to play a game to how many times a hitter grounded out to the shortstop. Many baseball stats date back to the late nineteenth and early twentieth century. Others, like saves and blown saves have come along in more recent years. Thanks to computers, stats can be kept on all sorts of things. Below are the most common player statistics that you will see in the sports pages. They are usually found for each game in what was termed back in the 1800s as a "box score," or a summary of the game in a box. Over one hundred years later, whether you find them in the newspaper or online, they are still the most popular way to see what happened in a ballgame.

Box Score

Below is a sample box score based on an actual game:

	1 2 3 4 5 6 7 8 9	R	H	E
San Francisco Giants	0 0 1 1 0 0 0 1 1	4	9	0
St. Louis Cardinals	0 0 0 2 0 0 0 0 0	2	9	0

Giants

	Pos	ab	r	h	rbi	bb	so	avg
Bernard	CF	4	0	0	0	0	2	.279
Davis	3B	3	1	1	0	0	1	.267
Bonds	LF	4	1	1	1	0	1	.323
Kent	2B	4	0	1	0	0	1	.354
Burks	RF	4	1	3	0	0	0	.351
Snow	1B	3	0	1	1	0	0	.296
Aurilia	SS	4	0	1	1	0	1	.265
Martinez	SS	0	0	0	0	0	0	.306
Mirabelli	C	3	0	0	0	1	0	.242
Rueter	P	3	0	0	0	0	0	.133
Murray	PH	1	1	1	1	0	0	.285
Embree	P	0	0	0	0	0	0	.000
Nen	P	0	0	0	0	0	0	.000
Totals		**33**	**4**	**9**	**4**	**1**	**6**	

Cardinals

	Pos	ab	r	h	rbi	bb	so	avg
Vina	2B	4	1	2	0	0	0	.289
Renteria	SS	3	0	0	0	0	1	.278
Edmonds	CF	4	1	1	2	0	0	.340
McGwire	1B	3	0	1	0	1	0	.305
Tatis	3B	4	0	3	0	0	0	.345
Lankford	LF	3	0	0	0	1	2	.239
Matheny	C	3	0	1	0	0	0	.250
Dunston	PH	1	0	0	0	0	1	.247
Drew	RF	4	0	1	0	0	0	.289
Kile	P	2	0	0	0	1	0	.129
Howard	PH	1	0	0	0	0	0	.194
Morris	P	0	0	0	0	0	0	.250
Totals		**32**	**2**	**9**	**2**	**3**	**4**	

Batting: 2B: Burks (12), Kent (21) HR: Bonds (27), Murray (5), RBI Bonds (65), Snow (41), Aurilia (32), Murray (19) Team LOB – 8
Baserunning: CS Mirabelli (2)
Fielding: DP: 1 (Kent-Aurilia-Snow)

Batting: 3B: Vina (4), HR: Edmonds (25)
RBI: Edmonds 2 (60) S- Renteria
Team LOB – 7
Baserunning: SB: Tatis (7)

Pitcher

	ip	h	r	er	bb	so	hr	era
Rueter	7⅓	8	2	2	2	1	1	3.67
Embree (W1-2)	⅔	1	0	0	0	1	0	5.18
Nen (S, 17)	1	0	0	0	1	2	0	2.29

Pitcher

	ip	h	r	er	bb	so	hr	era
Kile	7	6	2	2	1	4	1	4.32
Morris (L2-2)	2	3	2	2	0	2	1	2.95

Attendance: 46,005
Game Length: 3:11

FUN FACT

Ultimate Inning

In 1999, Fernando Tatis of the St. Louis Cardinals hit a grand slam home run. His team kept on hitting and scoring runs in the inning so that he got to bat again in the same inning with the bases loaded. Believe it or not, he hit another grand slam, becoming the first player ever to hit two grand slam home runs and drive in eight runs in one inning. Wow!

I'll Play Anywhere

Only two players in baseball history have played all ten positions. That's right, ten! Bert Campaneris of the A's and Cesar Tovar of the Twins not only played all nine positions, including one pitching appearance each, but they were also designated hitters.

BUT what does it all mean, you may wonder. Well, it's very simple.

Across the top is the inning-by-inning account of runs scored. You'll see that the Giants got one in the top of the third and another in the top of the fourth inning before the Cardinals got two in the bottom of the fourth. The innings are usually listed in groups of threes.

R, H, and E are runs, hits, and errors for each team for the game.

The rest of the abbreviations are as follows:
Pos is the position that player played. Sometimes a backup will take over at that position, like on the Giants' side where you see Aurilia at shortstop (ss) replaced by Martinez at shortstop (ss).

The positions are always:
1B	First base
2B	Second base
3B	Third base
SS	Shortstop
LF	Left fielder
CF	Center fielder
RF	Right fielder
C	Catcher
P	Pitcher
PH	Pinch hitter (someone who bats for another player, such as Murray or Howard in the game above)
PR	Pinch runner (someone who runs for someone else)
DH	In the American League and in some minor leagues there are Designated Hitters, who bat for the pitchers.

The rest of the stats tell you what the player did in the game.

ab   At bats, or how many times the batter officially had a turn at bat (walks, sacrifices, and being hit by a pitch don't count as official at bats)

r   Runs scored

h   Hits

rbi   Runs batted in (a hit or another play that brings in a run or more)

bb   Base on balls (or walks)

so   Strikeouts, also sometimes listed as "**k**"

avg   Batting average (the percentage of hits a player gets per at bats; .300 or better is the mark of a good hitter, meaning that 30 percent of the time he bats he gets a hit). Batting average is also listed as "**ba**."

There will also be some information listed underneath the line that says "totals," telling you who hit doubles (2B), triples (3B), and home runs (HR) and how many the player has for the season in each category. You'll also see if a player had a sacrifice (S) or a sacrifice fly (SF), where a runner scored from third base after that batter hit a flyball for an out. Players don't like to see it, but there is also a listing of errors (E) as well. Runs batted in (RBI) may be listed again with the number the player has for the season. Next to "Baserunning," stolen bases (SB) and caught stealing (CS) are also listed. Some box scores may give you more detailed information, but these are the basics.

Pitching statistics are also included. Commonly you'll find next to pitchers' names first the overall outcome, meaning win (W) or loss (L), plus saves (S) for a reliever. In the game above, Embree was the winning pitcher in relief of Rueter, and Nen

got the save, his seventeenth. Morris was the losing pitcher, also in relief. His win-loss record is listed as 2–2, or 2 wins and 2 losses for the season.

Other numbers you may see next to the name are:

bs Blown saves, and a number of how many the pitcher has blown.

h Hold–a new statistic will show up for relief pitchers that says they held the lead until the closer came in and finished the game.

Then you'll see what is called the "pitcher's line" for the game, which includes:

ip Innings pitched. Sometimes you'll see 6 1/3 or 6.3 meaning the pitcher lasted six innings and got one out in the seventh. 6 2/3 or 6.7 would mean two outs in the seventh.

h Hits allowed

r Runs allowed

er Earned runs allowed. A run can be scored that doesn't count as an "earned run" because there was an error on the play that put the runner on base who later scored or helped the runner to score. In the game above there were no errors, so there could not be any unearned runs.

bb Base on balls, or walks allowed

so Strikeouts (sometimes listed as "k")

hr How many home runs allowed

era The up-to-date earned run average of the pitcher, or how many earned runs he allows per nine innings. Pitchers try to keep their earned run averages under 4.00, which is getting harder to do in recent years. Under 3.50 is quite good and under 3.00 is excellent. Starting pitchers pitch more innings so it's harder for them to keep those ERAs down.

ACTIVITY

Calculating Batting Average

The best gauge of a hitter is batting average. It measures the number of times a ballplayer gets hits compared to the number of times the player bats. For example, if you bat 100 times and you get 30 hits, you're getting hits 30 percent of the time, and your batting average is .300. In baseball .300 and above is very good, while .200 might get you sent back to the minor leagues unless you're a terrific fielder. What's amazing is that in all the 100+ years of baseball, batting averages have always remained in a similar range in the major leagues. Sure, you might hit .600 in Little League, but at the professional level, .325 was a very good batting average in 1921, and it remains a good average in 2001.

To figure out batting average, divide the number of hits by the number of at bats. For example, 4 hits in 12 at bats would be 4 divided by 12, or .333. Remember, a base on balls, getting hit by a pitch, or a sacrifice does not count as a time at bat. Reaching base on an error does count as an at bat, but not as a hit. Therefore if you batted three times and once you grounded out, once you got a single and once you reached base on an error, you would have one hit in three at bats, or a batting average of .333 (1 divided by 3).

You may also see "**pc**," which is pitch count, indicating how many pitches the pitcher threw.

Millions of baseball fans love looking at box scores, which explains why this simple wrap up of the game has been popular for many decades.

Player Statistics

If you turn over baseball cards or look at numerous baseball books, including this one, you'll find ballplayers' statistics for each season and for their careers. The most commonly found stats for hitters include:

G	Games played
AB	At bats
R	Runs
H	Hits
2B	Doubles
3B	Triples
HR	Home runs
RBI	Runs batted in
BB	Base on balls
K or SO	Strikeouts
BA or AVG	Batting average
SB	Stolen bases
CS	Caught stealing

You might also see SLG, or slugging percentage, which takes 1 point for each single, 2 for each double, 3 for each triple, and 4 for each home run, adds them up and divides by the number of at bats.

Common pitching stats include:

W   Wins

L   Losses

PCT   This is winning percentage, or how often the pitcher gets a win versus a loss. Add together wins and losses, then take the number of wins and divide it by the number you get. For example, if a pitcher has a win-loss record of 10 wins and 2 losses, you would add 10 + 2 = 12. Then divide the 10 wins by 12 and you'll get .833, or a great winning percentage of .833!

G   Games pitched in

GS   Games started

CG   Complete games

Sho   Shutouts (held the opposing team to no runs)

IP   Innings pitched

Hits   Hits allowed

BB   Base on balls allowed

K or SO   Strikeouts

ERA   Earned run average

And for relief pitchers the most common two stats are:

S   Saves

BS   Blown saves

Beyond those found that we have listed, there are statistics kept for nearly everything, and you can find books that get more detailed depending on how much you love baseball statistics.

The same statistics listed for a player can also be found for a team, although individual stats are generally more popular in baseball. In football, team stats are more widely looked at since it is a less individual game. Baseball is pitcher versus hitter.

WORDS to KNOW

Wild Card: In major league baseball there are three divisions in each league, but four teams make the play-offs each year. The fourth team, the wild card team, is the team in each league with the next best record, or the best second-place team from any one of the three divisions.

The Standings

To follow your favorite team, you can look in the newspaper at the sports pages or on a Web site like *www.majorleaguebaseball.com* or *www.sportingnews.com* and you can get plenty of information including the standings, the listings of who's in first place, second place, and so on.

The major leagues today are each broken into three divisions:

American League

East	Central	West
Baltimore Orioles	Chicago White Sox	Anaheim Angels
Boston Red Sox	Cleveland Indians	Oakland Athletics
New York Yankees	Detroit Tigers	Seattle Mariners
Tampa Bay Devil Rays	Kansas City Royals	Texas Rangers
Toronto Blue Jays	Minnesota Twins	

National League

East	Central	West
Atlanta Braves	Chicago Cubs	Arizona Diamondbacks
Florida Marlins	Cincinnati Reds	Colorado Rockies
Montreal Expos	Houston Astros	Los Angeles Dodgers
New York Mets	Milwaukee Brewers	San Diego Padres
Philadelphia Phillies	Pittsburgh Pirates	San Francisco Giants
	St. Louis Cardinals	

When you look at the standings in the papers, you'll see how many wins and losses the team has and their winning percentage, meaning what percentage of all the games they've played they've won.

Games Back

When you look at the standings, you will also see the abbreviation "GB" (games back), which is a very important way of judging how close your team is to first place in their division. Games back means how many games a team is behind the first place team. You might see:

	W L	GB
New York Yankees	60-40	——
Boston Red Sox	58-42	2
Baltimore Orioles	54-48	7
Toronto Blue Jays	49-50	?
Tampa Bay Devil Rays	40-60	?

How is this figured out?

Well, it's simple. You subtract how many games the teams are apart in wins and then do the same for losses. In the first example, you can figure out the difference between the Yankees and Red Sox.

In wins you have $60 - 58 = 2$.

In losses you have $42 - 40 = 2$.

Then add the two numbers you came up with together: $2 + 2 = 4$.

Then divide by 2: $4 \div 2 = 2$.

The Red Sox are therefore 2 games behind the Yankees.

That one was easy because they were 2 apart in wins and in losses. Sometimes, teams have played different numbers of games at a certain time in the season because of their schedules and because sometimes games are rained out (cancelled).

To see how many games back the Orioles are behind the Yankees, you would use the same formula.

Back to Back!

The only pitcher to ever throw two consecutive no-hitters was Johnny Vander Meer of the Cincinnati Reds in 1938.

Four Home Runs

When a player hits two home runs in a game it's considered a great game, three home runs is very rare, but four homers in one game!? It's been done just nine times in baseball history (in a nine-inning game) going back to 1894. Willie Mays did it, but Babe Ruth never did, and neither has McGwire—yet.

Wins, 60 – 54 = 6.

Losses, 48 – 40 = 8.

Then add them together: 6 + 8 = 14.

Then divide by 2: 14 ÷ 2 = 7.

The Orioles are 7 games behind the Yankees.

Now, without looking below, try to figure out how far the Blue Jays are behind the Yankees.

Wins, 60 – 49 = 11.

Losses, 50 – 40 = 10.

11 + 10 = 21.

21 divided by 2 = 10½.

Now you try Tampa Bay!

(In case you're wondering, the answer to the question above is that Tampa Bay is 20 games out.)

Record Holders and Top 10 Lists

As mentioned earlier, there are statistics kept for everything in baseball. You could probably find the answer to "What pitcher threw the most wild pitches in night games at Wrigley Field in the 1940s?" Okay, so that's a trick question—there were no night games at Wrigley in the 1940s because they had no lights. The point is, however, that if you love statistics you could probably spend a year looking at baseball statistics and never see the same one twice.

Following are some favorites.

All-Time Record Holders

Hitting

Top 10 All-Time Home Run Leaders

1. Hank Aaron 755
2. Babe Ruth 714
3. Willie Mays 660
4. Frank Robinson 586
5. Harmon Killebrew 573
6. Reggie Jackson 563
7. Mark McGwire 554*
8. Mike Schmidt 548
9. Mickey Mantle 536
10. Jimmie Foxx 534

*The currently active leader is Mark McGwire.

There are 16 players who have topped 500 home runs in their careers and Barry Bonds is getting close to becoming number 17.

Top 10 All-Time RBI Leaders

1. Hank Aaron 2,297
2. Babe Ruth 2,212
3. Lou Gehrig 1,995
4. Ty Cobb 1,961
5. Stan Musial 1,951
6. Jimmie Foxx 1,921
7. Eddie Murray 1,917
8. Willie Mays 1,903
9. Mel Ott 1,860
10. Carl Yastrzemski 1,844

Top 11 Batting Average Leaders (more than 5,000 at bats)

1. Ty Cobb .367
2. Rogers Hornsby .358
3. Dan Brouthers .349
4. Ed Delahanty .346
5. Willie Keeler .345
   Tris Speaker .345
7. Billy Hamilton .344
   Ted Williams .344
9. Jesse Burkett .342
   Harry Heilmann .342
   Babe Ruth .342

The Most Hits: Pete Rose at 4,256, followed by Ty Cobb at 4,191. They are the only two with over 4,000 hits!

The Most Grand Slam Home Runs: Lou Gehrig 23

The Most Stolen Bases: Rickey Henderson 1,370

The Most At Bats: Pete Rose 14,053

Most Seasons Played: Nolan Ryan 27

Pitching

Top 11 All-Time Wins Leaders

1. Cy Young 511
2. Walter Johnson 417
3. Pete Alexander 373
   Christy Mathewson 373
5. Warren Spahn 363
6. Pud Gavin 361
   Kid Nichols 361

Baseball Diamond

Can you find six common baseball terms hidden in the diamond grid? Start at a letter and move one space at a time in any direction to a touching letter. You may not use the same letter twice in a word, but you can cross over your own path. HINT: One of the terms is an abbreviation!

Hidden Words

1. _____
2. _____
3. _____
4. _____
5. _____
6. _____

8. Tim Keefe 344
9. Steve Carlton 329
10. John Clarkson 326
    Eddie Plank 326

Top 10 All-Time Strikeout Leaders

1. Nolan Ryan 5,174
2. Steve Carlton 4,136
3. Bert Blyleven 3,701
4. Tom Seaver 3,640
5. Don Sutton 3,574
6. Gaylord Perry 3,534
7. Walter Johnson 3,508
8. Roger Clemens 3,504*
9. Phil Niekro 3,316
10. Ferguson Jenkins 3,192

*Active player total through the 2000 season. Randy Johnson just topped 3,000 in the year 2000 and is still going strong.

Lowest All-Time ERA: (2,000 or more innings)
Ed Walsh 1.82

Most All-Time Saves: Lee Smith 478 (since 1969 when saves became an "official" statistic)

Most No-Hitters: Nolan Ryan 7

One Season Records

Hitting

Most Doubles: Earl Webb 67, Boston Red Sox 1931

Most Triples: Owen Wilson 36, Pittsurgh Pirates 1912

Most Home Runs: Mark McGwire 70, St. Louis Cardinals 1998

Sammy Sosa 66, Chicago Cubs 1998

Mark McGwire 65, St Louis Cardinals 1999

Sammy Sosa 63, Chicago Cubs 1999

Roger Maris 61, New York Yankees 1961

Babe Ruth 60, New York Yankees 1927

Babe Ruth 59, New York Yankees 1921

Jimmie Foxx 58, Philadelphia Athletics 1932

Hank Greenberg 58, Detroit Tigers 1938

Mark McGwire 58, Oakland A's/St. Louis Cardinals 1997

Most Grand Slam Home Runs: Don Mattingly 6, New York Yankees 1987

Most Runs Batted In: Hack Wilson 191, Chicago Cubs 1930

Most Hits: George Sisler 257, St. Louis Browns 1920

Highest Batting Average (500+ Plate Appearances): Hugh Duffy .438, 1894

Highest Average (500+ Plate Appearances) since 1900: Rogers Hornsby .424, St. Louis Cardinals 1924

Most Stolen Bases: Rickey Henderson 130, Oakland Athletics 1982

Pitching

Most Wins: Jack Chesbro 41, New York Highlanders 1904

Most Strikeouts: Nolan Ryan 383, California Angels 1973

Lowest Earned Run Average: Dutch Leonard 1.01, Boston Red Sox 1914

Must Shutouts: Grover Alexander 16, Philadelphia Phillies 1916

Most Saves: Bobby Thigpen 57, Chicago White Sox 1990

FUN FACT

Manager Wins

The manager with the most all-time wins is Connie Mack, who won 3,731 games over 53 years between between 1894 and 1950. (He lost over 4,000.)

Longest Batting Streaks

In 1941 Joe DiMaggio got hits in an incredible 56 consecutive games, a record that has held up for 60 years. After the hitting streak ended, DiMaggio hit safely in another 16 games, giving him hits in 72 of 73 games. Wow! The next longest hitting streaks, and two longest in the National League, were by Willie Keeler way back in 1897 and Pete Rose in 1978. Both hit in 44 consecutive games!

Playing Card Baseball Solitaire

My dad invented this game years ago, way before computers and Game Boy. It's a fun game for a rainy day or when you're home sick or even on vacation. It's a nice change from computer games that doesn't involve computer graphics or any other equipment. All you need is a piece of paper, a pen or pencil, and a deck of cards—the excitement goes on in your imagination as you play. It also helps to know how to score the game (see the chapter on scoring).

First you write down two lineups of nine players each. Then you can play a game of Card Baseball.

Shuffle the deck and turn over three cards. The third card is what the batter does. You turn over three per hitter until there are three outs. Shuffle the deck and the other team comes up—you do the same for the other team. Score as you go if you know how, or in any manner you like.

The Cards:

- 2, 3, 4, 5, 6, 7, and red 9s are outs
- Black 9s are walks
- 10s are strikeouts
- Jacks are singles, red Jacks move base runners 2 bases, black Jacks move base runners one base.
- Queens are doubles, red Queens let base runners on second score, black Queens mean they go to third.
- Red Kings are triples, black Kings are like black Jacks—they are singles (because there aren't too many triples hit in baseball).
- Aces are home runs.

You can make one card in the deck an error card, meaning the batter reached a base on an error.

For a game with high scoring use all 52 cards (no jokers needed). For a game with lower scoring, take out a couple of Aces and one of the two red Kings. After every half inning shuffle the deck so the other team has the same chance to get all the possible hits.

One fun thing to do is to keep score of a baseball game. Scorecards are sold at the ballpark, or you can make your own on a sheet of paper. To make life a little easier, there is one provided in this book you can use as a model. The most important thing is that you have a place to write the name of each player and boxes for all nine innings (or more) so that you can put down what they do with each at bat. Names run down the left side of the page and innings run across the top. Why not try scoring the next game you go to?

Scoring Symbols

Scoring is really pretty easy once you know the symbols to put in the boxes. You are writing down what the batter does each time he bats. Most of the time you will be listing hits or outs. When the batter makes an out it is either hit to a fielder or a strikeout. For scoring purposes, the fielders are numbered—it has nothing to do with the numbers they are wearing on their uniforms.

Numbers for fielding:
1   Pitcher
2   Catcher
3   First baseman
4   Second baseman
5   Third baseman

6   Shortstop
7   Left fielder
8   Center fielder
9   Right fielder

You then write the number of the player or players who caught the ball to get the batter out. For example, if the ball is hit in the air to the center fielder and he makes the catch for an out, you put "8" in the box. If the ball went to right field, you'd put "9," or to left field, "7." If the player pops it up or hits a line drive and it's caught by the first baseman, you'd put "3," or for the second baseman you'd put "4," and so on.

If the ball is hit on the ground to the shortstop and he throws to first, you put down both numbers since they were both part of the play. Therefore a groundout to shortstop would be 6-3. A groundout to second base would be 4-3, a groundout to third base 5-3. If the first baseman picked up a groundball and the pitcher came over to cover first base, caught the throw, and stepped on the base for the out, it would be scored 3-1, because the first baseman is "3" and the pitcher is "1." A double play that goes from the shortstop to the second baseman to the first baseman would be scored as 6-4-3.

Whatever fielders are involved in making the out are included in your scoring. Once you memorize the fielders' numbers it becomes very easy.

Hits can be scored in a few ways. A single is either "1B" or a single line (–), a double is "2B" or a double line (=), a triple is 3B or a triple line (≡), and a home run is "HR" or four lines (≡) (Most people, even those who use lines for other hits, like to put HR for a home run—it looks more impressive than four lines.)

As runners get on base you then keep track of them using the diamond in the box on the scorecard.

WORDS to KNOW

Pickoff: If there's a base runner and the pitcher throws to the fielder, who catches the runner off base and tags that runner for an out, it's called a pickoff. A pickoff at first base would be scored in the corner next to how the runner got on first base: PO 1-3, pickoff, pitcher to first base.

Scoring Position: When a runner is on second or third base, he is considered in scoring position, meaning it's easier to score on a hit.

WORDS to KNOW

Intentional Walk: An intentional walk, sometimes called an intentional pass, is when a pitcher walks a batter on purpose. Sometimes this makes it easier to get a doubleplay if there are other runners on second and/or third. Sometimes a batter is walked intentionally because the player is very good and the pitcher doesn't want to give up a home run. It is scored as "IW" or "IBB."

Assist: When a player makes a throw of any kind to get an out, whether it's an infielder throwing a batter out running to first base or an outfielder throwing a runner out at home plate, the player gets an assist.

Just draw on the line for each base they get to. For example, if a player reaches first base you would draw on the line going from home to first base. If the next player gets a single and that player moves to second base you would darken the line going from first base to second base.

As the players move around the bases you draw the lines of the diamond to follow them. Therefore, for every run scored you would have a complete diamond. Some people score on the outside of the diamond. Others score inside the diamond.

There are many many variations on scoring. Sportswriters, broadcasters, fans, and people who are keeping the statistics for the team are all keeping score, and they're all doing it in a slightly different manner from each other. Since there are so many ways to score, there are actually 50 different types of scorecards printed. As long as you can follow what is going on in the game, and you are having fun, that's all that really matters.

Other Scoring Symbols for Hitters

BB   Base on balls

K   Strikeout

     If the batter struck out looking (meaning he just stood there while the umpire called a pitch over home plate for strike three) then you can put a backwards K or ꓘ.

HBP   Hit by pitch

SF   Sacrifice fly

S or SAC   Sacrifice bunt (when the batter bunts the ball just to move the runner over to second or third base)

Score!

Follow the directions below to color in this scorecard and find out the answer to the following riddle: What kind of baseball players live in the North Pole?

> Great! A triple play!

1. Color in all the boxes scoring a single.
2. Color in all the boxes scoring singles where the runner made it to second base.
3. Color in all the boxes scoring doubles where the runner made it to third base.
4. Color in all the boxes scoring singles where a run was completed.
5. Color in all the boxes scoring strikeouts.
6. Color in all the boxes scoring home runs.

Players	1	2	3	4	5	6	7	8	9	10	11	AB	R	H	RBI
Rose (5)	→	⬦	→	⬦	K	→	→		→	E3		→	→	→	S
Morgan (4)	HR		→		→	S	⬦	E3	→		⬦	W	→		→
Bench (2)	⬦	→	E3	→	K	E3	→		K	→	E3		→	→	⬦
Perez (3)	→	→	K		→	→	HR		→	K	→	W	→	→	→
Foster (7)		→	E3	W		⬦	W		S	→		E3	→		→
Griffey (9)	→	K	⬦		→	→		⬦	W	→	⬦		K	→	K
Geronimo (8)	→	S	⬦	→	K	→	⬦	→		⬦		→	HR		⬦
Gullet (1)	K	E3	→		→		→	K	⬦	→	K	⬦		→	
Carroll (6)	→	W	⬦	W	K	E3		⬦	⬦	→			E3		⬦
McEnaney (10)	⬦	K	⬦	→	⬦		E3	→		→	K	→	K	→	→

E#   Error, followed by the number of the fielder that made the error. An error on the first baseman, for example, would be E3.

DP   Double play (including the fielders numbers involved in the play)

TP   Triple play (including the fielders numbers involved in the play)

Triple plays are extremely rare, so if you score one of these, save the scorecard.

GS   Grand slam home run! The biggest hit in baseball.

Say What?

Yogi Berra is known as being quite a talker behind the plate. He hoped his chatter would distract the batter! The story goes that in the 1958 World Series, with the legendary Hank Aaron hitting, Yogi kept telling Hank to "hit with the label up on the bat." Finally, Hank couldn't stand it any more. He turned to Yogi and said

"_____!"

C'mon Hank, hit it with the label up. Up, up, up. With the label up. C'mon Hank, hit it with the label up...

To find out what Hank Aaron said to Yogi Berra, figure out where to put each of the scrambled letters. The letters all fit in the boxes under their own column.

Y	O		H		I		N	O	M			O		R	E			
T	O	G	I	I	T		C	A	T	E	T	H	E	R	E	A	D	
				,														
					,												!	

Runner's Symbols

Other symbols you might use that don't describe what the batter did, but often tell you that the runners moved up, can be put in a corner of the box:

SB   Stolen base

   This goes next to the player who stole the base.

CS   Caught stealing

   This goes next to the runner thrown out stealing.

PB   Passed ball

WP   Wild pitch

E   Error

   If, for example, a catcher tried to throw a runner out stealing second base or a pitcher tried to pick a runner off first, and they threw the ball past the base allowing the runners to move up a base, you would put E2 or E1 to indicate the runner moved up on an error.

Baseball Questions and Answers

How Do You Determine the Winning Pitcher?

When a team wins a game, how do you know who the winning pitcher is when more than one pitcher played for the team?

Every game has a winning and losing pitcher. The winning pitcher is the pitcher who was playing for the winning team at the time they took the lead and did not lose the lead again.

For example, if Pedro Martinez starts a game for the Red Sox against the Indians and the Red Sox take a 4–0 lead in the

Four Strikeouts in an Inning?

Yes, it's possible to get four, or even more strikeouts in the same half of an inning. Whenever there is a strikeout, the catcher must hold onto the ball. If the catcher drops the ball on the third strike, the batter can run to first base. The catcher must complete the play by throwing to first base. Almost every time, the catcher will simply throw the ball to the first baseman for the out. However, if the catcher makes a bad throw to first, the runner could be safe. It's actually happened where a pitcher has struck out four batters in an inning because one reached base on a catcher's error. Yes, the pitcher and the hitter both get credit for a strikeout in the stats. Score it K-E2 (strikeout and error on the catcher for letting the batter get to base).

The Magic Number

Near the end of the baseball season, teams start to figure out the "magic number." This is how many games the leading team must win, and how many games any other team must lose, for the leader to win the pennant (championship in their league).

Put on your thinking cap, because there's some tricky math here. Pretend you have two teams — Team A and Team B. Team A is the leading team in the league, having won the most games so far. Team B is any other team in the league.

Step 1: ADD the number of games Team B has won and the number of games Team B has left to play
Step 2: SUBTRACT the number of games Team A has won
Step 3: ADD the number 1

The answer is the "magic number," or the number of games that Team A must win in order to beat Team B for the pennant.

Here's a sample for you to try.

The season has 162 scheduled games.		
	won	lost
TEAM A	93	59
TEAM B	89	63
games TEAM B has won		_____
ADD games TEAM B has left		_____
		_____
SUBTRACT games TEAM A has won		_____
		_____
ADD the number 1		_____
THE MAGIC NUMBER		_____

early innings and go on to win the game 4–3, Martinez will be the winning pitcher since they never gave up the lead.

However, if the Indians come back and tie the game and the Red Sox bring in a relief pitcher in the seventh inning and then score two runs in the eighth and win 6–4, the relief pitcher would get the win because he was the pitcher when his team took the lead and didn't lose it again.

Starting pitchers get more wins because they pitch more innings. A starting pitcher must go five innings to get a win.

Losing pitchers are determined in the opposite way. If a pitcher gives up the runs that put the other team ahead and his team never catches up, then he gets the loss.

New Pitcher or Pitching Change

You might draw a line between the batters' boxes where a new pitcher came into the ballgame.

What Does the "Official Scorer" Do?

The official scorer is someone at every game (often a sports journalist) whose job is to decide on how to score certain plays. They will decide if a ball hit that a fielder drops or throws badly is a hit or an error. Official scorers also decide other plays, such as a wild pitch, which means the pitcher threw a really bad pitch, or a passed ball, which means the pitch got past the catcher, but it was the catcher's error and not a wild throw by the pitcher.

When Was the First Scorecard Used?

The first scorecard was created by the Knickerbocker ball club way back in 1845.

WORDS to KNOW

Putout: Whenever a fielder catches a ball that results in an out, it's a putout. This includes a first baseman taking a throw from an infielder and stepping on the base, or a catcher on a strikeout.

Walk-Off Home Run: A new term, this refers to a home run in the bottom of the ninth or in the home team's at bat in the bottom of an extra inning that wins and ends the game. Following the home run, the teams walk off the field—hence the name.

Why do the managers and umpires meet at home plate before every game?

You may notice that before each game there is a short meeting between the umpires and the managers or coaches. This is to discuss the ground rules. Every stadium is built differently, and it's important that everyone understands the specific rules for what is considered in-play and what is foul territory. Some ballparks have a line on a high fence. If the ball is over that line it's a home run. Other stadiums have a high wall, but the rule is if it hits the wall, it's not a home run but still in play. Everything about the field needs to be talked about so there are no problems with the rules during the game. You probably do the same thing before playing any game with your friends, when you stop and go over the rules.

Inning 9

Baseball Cards

Fun Fact: The Most Valuable Card Ever

In case you're wondering about the most valuable card of all time, it's the 1909 Honus Wagner card, known to collectors as T-206. Honus did not want kids seeing his card associated with cigarettes, so he asked that the company stop printing his cards. Therefore, only a few cards of this legendary player exist. The card is now so rare that at an auction in New York City it sold for $640,000! Wow!

Collecting baseball cards can be a marvelous hobby. Cards come in packs of seven, ten, twelve, or more depending on the company and the type of pack you buy. Many companies make baseball cards, each with a different look. Topps, Donruss, Fleer, and Upper Deck are among the most popular card-making companies. The fun is seeing which player you get when you open the pack. You can try to collect your favorite players, get the biggest stars in the game, collect all the players on your favorite team(s), or try to get the entire set of cards for the season. If you've saved up your allowance or perhaps ask for it for a birthday gift, you can get a box of all the cards by one card company for the entire season. New cards come out every season, as they have since the early 1900s.

Most card buyers enjoy collecting the cards for the fun of it. The cards themselves have a glossy look and the photos are sometimes really cool action shots from the game. The statistics on the back of the cards give you all sorts of information about how the player has done in his career. It's a great hobby and one shared by millions of people. There are also more serious collectors who buy and sell older or more valuable cards for lots of money. Card shows, online card dealers, and auctions are places where adults who are in the baseball card business can buy and sell valuable cards. Buying cards online, however, is for more serious, grown-up collectors.

Some Baseball Card History

Professional baseball began at the end of the 1860s, and by the late 1880s the first baseball cards were printed. These early cards were printed on the cardboard backs of cigarette packs. Top players of the day like Cap Anson and Buck Ewing were among the first players to appear on cards. Pretty soon, in the early 1900s a number of cigarette manufacturers were printing cards of the best players, such as Ty Cobb and Honus Wagner. There were far fewer copies of each card printed then there are of cards today.

By the 1930s chewing gum companies were also making baseball cards, and collecting these cards was becoming more popular. In 1933 the Goudey Chewing Gum Company accidentally forgot to print card number 106 in their set, a card of all-star (and future Hall of Famer) Napoleon LaJoie. So many collectors sent letters asking for the missing card that the company had to print more in 1934, and it sent them to the people who had written in. This was one of the first indications that card collecting was becoming popular.

Then, in 1952, Topps made its first baseball cards with statistics of the players on the back. Through the 1960s and '70s card collecting was very popular, but it

Collectible Card

Sometimes the most valuable cards are those that accidentally get printed with a few mistakes or differences. Can you find the nine differences between these two cards?

WORDS to KNOW

Commons: Commons are cards that don't have much value because they are only average players. This is the category where most cards fall, but they still may have value to you as a favorite player or a player on your favorite team.

wasn't until the late 1980s that rich collectors began to pay high prices for old cards, and baseball cards were seen as an investment, like putting money in the stock market. Today, card collecting isn't quite as popular as it was at the start of the 1990s, but it is still very popular. There are plenty of magazines and books about baseball card collecting. Becketts is a leading company in the business of making pricing guides and magazines about card collecting. If you have a growing card collection, it can be fun to see which cards are worth a few dollars. You might want to save up some of your allowance and buy some cards of star players from recent seasons. Perhaps a rookie card of a current star. Be careful and look at the price guides so you'll know what the going rate should be and you don't get ripped off.

Card shows are fun places to look at old and new cards and to meet other people who are collectors. It's a place where you might find a card or two that you can afford to buy, but first make sure it's okay with your parents . . . and don't spend too much money to start a hobby. Remember, the cards you buy in a pack today may be just as valuable in several years if you get players who are or become stars.

Stick of Gum

Once upon a time, one of the things you would always find in a pack of baseball cards was a long, pink stick of chewing gum. This isn't very common anymore, but it was standard with cards for many years.

Why Are Some Cards More Valuable Than Others?

For one thing, the greater players are more valuable because everyone knows them. Older cards, like those from the 1940s, '50s or '60s are usually more valuable than cards from the '70s or '80s because they are harder to find. Not as many people saved them, so they are considered more valuable since there aren't too many around. When a lot of people want something, like a

valuable card, the person who owns it can ask for more money since people can't go out and find that card elsewhere.

Cards that have a "defect," or an error, on them are also valuable since they are very rare and usually the error was corrected by the company after they printed the first few. Sometimes a word is off center or even spelled wrong. A couple of times a company printed the wrong name on the wrong picture. Now that's a big mistake—and a valuable card.

Sometimes it might depend on where you are selling a card. For example, in Boston a Nomar Garciapara rookie card is more valuable or would sell for more than in New York because he is a Red Sox fan favorite. In New York, however a Derek Jeter card would be more valuable than in Boston because he is a Yankee.

If a player is heading to the Hall of Fame, his card will be more valuable since that is baseball's greatest honor and very few players get there.

Rookie Cards

Often the most valuable card of a player is his rookie card, which is the first card put out for that player by a major card company that is licensed to distribute cards. A company that is licensed means that they have permission by Major League Baseball to print cards. You never know who's going to be the next Barry Bonds or Ken Griffey Jr., so if you have a rookie card hold onto it. It's fun to get rookie cards of players and root for them to become stars. It doesn't happen often, but you never know. Hang onto those rookie cards.

Take Good Care of Your Cards

It's important for any kind of collector, whether it's stamps or baseball cards, to take good care of their collection. Binders with plastic pages for sliding cards in and displaying them are one good way to save your best cards and keep them in good shape. Other people keep their cards in shoe boxes or other safe places. Try not to bend the cards or curl the corners. Cards that are in very good to excellent condition are worth more (and look better) than cards that are bent or not in good shape. Also, don't keep cards in places that are damp, cold, or very hot, and don't keep them in tight rubber bands that will cut into the cards.

Activities

MLB Showdown

It's a very hot game for baseball fans of all ages. This is a baseball card game sold in stores that lets you buy more baseball cards to add to the fun. The cards are also being listed in card collecting magazines as collectibles. For $10 to $12 you can buy the MLB Showdown Card Game, which has two 12-player teams, two 20-card strategy decks, a play mat, rule book, and multisided die. That's all you need to get into this very hot, popular new game. You have a roster of players, make a lineup, keep score, and most of all have fun. You can then buy additional packs of the cards to add more players to your roster.

    The game comes with three levels of play, so it works for young kids age six or seven as well as teens, and even grownups are getting into it.

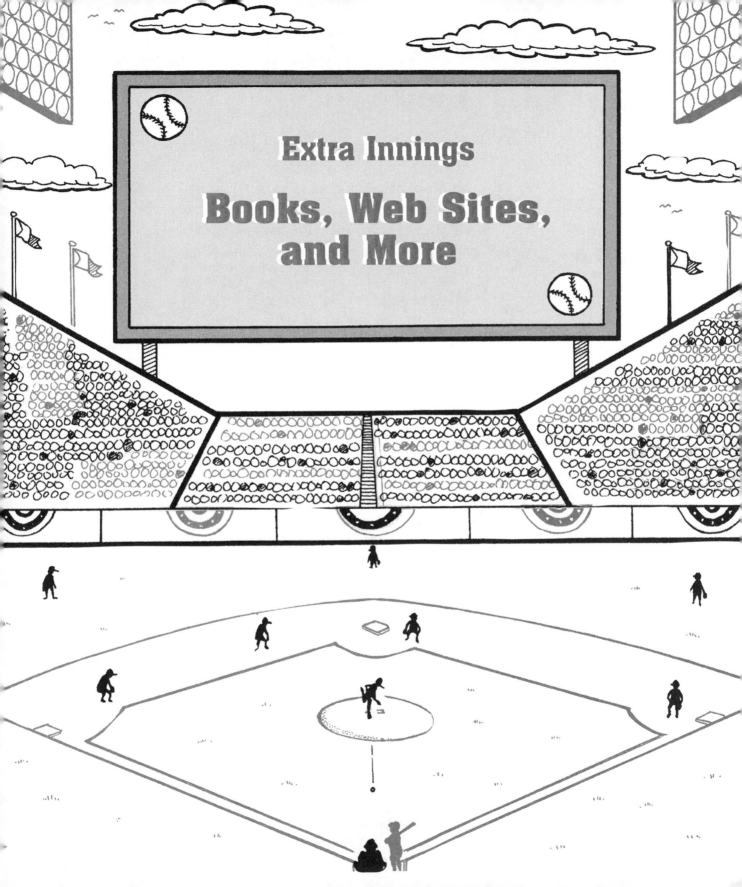

Extra Innings

Books, Web Sites, and More

FUN FACT

Player Plays Player

Did you know that Pete Rose played Ty Cobb in a movie about Babe Ruth? Confusing isn't it?

Duh!

According to the *Chicago Tribune*, the following statistic was given in the press notes for a Chicago-Oakland game: "The Oakland Athletics are 32-0 in games in which they have scored more runs than their opponents."

On Superstitions

Babe Ruth once said: "I only have one [superstition], whenever I hit a home run I make certain to touch all four bases."

Baseball Books

There are enough baseball books to fill a library, and if you go to the Hall of Fame in Cooperstown you'll actually find a library of baseball books. For the most part, baseball books fall into four main categories. Below is a brief description of what those categories are and a sample of what you can expect to find in each.

Historical

There are lots of books filled with stories about the history of the game. These books are often written by players, broadcasters, or sportswriters. These books provide a look at how baseball was played over the years and many of the great players who played it. They often have neat photos of early players and old-time stadiums. You can compare how the game looked then to how it looks today.

Here are a few:

The Sporting News Selects: Baseball's 25 Greatest Moments by Ron Smith and Joe Morgan

The All-Century Team by Mark Vancil looks at the 100 best players of the twentieth century.

The 500 Home Run Club by Bob Allen looks at the 16 greatest home run hitters, from Ruth to McGwire.

The Story of The Negro Leagues by William Brashler has the history and the stars of these leagues.

300 Great Baseball Cards of the 20th Century is a historical look at baseball cards from Beckett Publishing.

How to Play the Game

Many great players, coaches, and managers have written books telling their secrets on hitting, running, fielding, and pitching. How-to books might just give you an edge over the competition when you go out and play.

Here are a few such books:

Jeff Burroughs's Little League Instructional Guide

Baseball for Kids: Skills, Strategies and Stories to Make You a Better Ballplayer by Jerry Kasoff

Touching All the Bases: Baseball for Kids of All Ages by Claire MacKay

The Art of Pitching by Tom Seaver

The Art of Hitting by Tony Gwynn

The Science of Hitting by Ted Williams is a classic book on how to hit.

Biographies

Sometimes it's fun to see how a star made it to the big leagues and what it's like being a baseball star. Almost every great player, past and present, has a book out. There are many that are part of a larger series of books on several players.

Here are just a few:

At the Plate with Mark McGwire, *At the Plate with Sammy Sosa*, and *At the Plate with Ken Griffey* by Matt Christopher

Alex Rodriguez: Gunning for Greatness is one of several books on the great young shortstop.

Jackie and Me (about Jackie Robinson), *Babe and Me*, and *Honus and Me* (about Honus Wagner) are in the Baseball Card Adventure series by Dan Gutman.

Lou Gehrig, Pride of the Yankees by Keith Brandt

Babe Ruth, Home Run Hero by Keith Brandt

Baseball Films

It seems that every year another baseball movie comes out. Many haven't been big box office hits, but a few have been successful, and some are great fun to rent. Here are a few of the all-time best baseball films:

The Pride of the Yankees, 1942, The Lou Gehrig Story

The Babe Ruth Story, 1948

The Jackie Robinson Story, 1950

Angels in the Outfield, 1951, the original

Damn Yankees, 1958

Bang the Drum Slowly, 1973

The Bad News Bears, 1976

The Natural, 1984

Field of Dreams, 1989

Major League, 1989

A League of Their Own, 1992, about the women's leagues of the 1940s

Angels in the Outfield, 1994, the remake

Extra In-nings

Use the clue underneath the colored box to come up with a word. Write this word in the box.
When you add the word "IN," the new word has a totally different meaning!

1. _____ I N = to start
   (to plead for money)

2. _____ I N = a small house in the woods
   (taxi)

3. _____ I N = a springtime bird with a red breast
   (steal)

4. _____ I N = a heavy, shiny fabric
   (past tense of sit)

5. _____ I N = penguin-like bird with a colorful beak
   (short breath out)

> This game goes on, and on, and on!

Lists, Quotes, Jokes, and Statistics Books

Huh?

"On father's day we once again wish you all happy birthday."

—Mets broadcaster Ralph Kiner

There are plenty of books that compile lots of information. Some list jokes, others quotes, and plenty give you statistics. If you want information about any part of the game, you can find it.

Here are just a few examples:

Yogisms: I Didn't Really Say Everything I Said by Yogi Berra has a lot of the funniest sayings by one funny former catcher.

Total Baseball: The Official Encyclopedia of Major League Baseball by John Thorn is loaded with statistics and very heavy.

Baseball Card Price Guide from Sports Collectors Digest
Beckett Baseball Card Price Guide from Beckett Publishing
Batter Up! Baseball Activities for Kids of All Ages by Ouisie Shapiro

You can even work on your math skills and have some fun with *Baseball Math: Grandslam Activities and Projects for Grades 4–8* by Christopher Jennison.

Magazines

When you check out your local newsstand, if you look carefully, you may find newspapers or magazines about local teams. Below are a few national magazines and newspapers that you may look for that will keep you up to date on baseball.

Baseball Digest is a monthly magazine with stories about pro players past and present, rosters, a quiz (it's not easy), a crossword puzzle, and plenty of fun facts about the game.

Baseball Weekly is a magazine devoted to the latest info on the major leagues and even the minor leagues. Plenty of statistics and recent box scores are included in *Baseball Weekly*.

Junior League Baseball is all about baseball leagues for players 7 to 17.

The Sporting News is the weekly newspaper of all sports. During the spring and summer months, there are plenty of stories about baseball plus lots of neat stats.

Sports Illustrated for Kids has info on many sports, including baseball. The magazine includes stuff about playing the game and about your favorite players.

USA Today has a great sports section with a lot about baseball, including daily reports on each team so you can see what your favorite team is up to.

The President Is Here

The first U.S. president to attend a major league baseball game was Benjamin Harrison in 1892.

Presidential Toss

The tradition of having the president throw out the first pitch of the season in a pregame ceremony began in 1910 when President Taft threw out the opening pitch to Walter Johnson.

First V.P.

The first vice president to throw out the first pitch of the season in a pregame ceremony was Vice President Sherman in 1912. President Taft could not attend that day because of a tragedy, the sinking of the *Titanic*.

Baseball Online

There are many Web sites available now that give you access to all kinds of baseball information. A few are listed here with a description of what you can find.

www.sportingnews.com is home of the *Sporting News*, one of the leading sports newspapers for many years. If you click on MLB (Major League Baseball) in the upper left on the main page, you'll get the baseball page. You'll find headline news plus a long list on the left-hand side of places you can click on to give you more information, including standings, a scoreboard with up-to-the-inning game info, player bios, team reports, fun and prizes, and much more. The *Sporting News* site covers all the other major sports as well.

www.fastball.com has plenty of up-to-date information including the latest scores, pitching match-ups, and even the weather conditions for the games. There is plenty of baseball news, information on who's injured, current leaders, guest chats, standings, and more. The clubhouse store sells major league baseball clothing and plenty of cool stuff, but you'll need to get your parents' permission before purchasing.

www.usatoday.com/sports/mlb.htm is the home of *USA Today*'s baseball Web site. You can simply type in *www.usatoday.com* and click on baseball in the left-hand column. All the latest scores and info on the day's games are available plus loads of statistics, team schedules, TV schedules, injury reports, pitching match-ups, team reports, and lots of stuff to buy. Ask your parents before buying anything.

www.blackbaseball.com is a very informative site about the Negro Leagues. The history, players, teams, and a store with books (ask your parents before buying anything) are all part of this interesting site. There are new books featured and several articles that offer a lot of information on Jackie Robinson and on baseball's color barrier that kept African-American players out of the major leagues.

www.negroleaguebaseball.com is a similar site also featuring plenty of information on the Negro Leagues including books and articles.

www.baseball.com has all the latest up-to-the-inning scores, standings, statistics, trades, pitching match-ups, fantasy league info, minor league stats, and baseball news. It also has a link to the Web sites of each major league team. These sites are a lot of fun to check out.

www.majorleaguebaseball.com is the major league's official baseball Web site. You can find anything you need there, including up-to-the-inning scores, pitching match-ups for the next several days, injury reports, trades, news, player statistics for every major leaguer, plus info on everything from spring training through the World Series. There is a history section with links to all sorts of baseball records and much, much more. If it has anything to do with major league baseball you'll find it here! In May and June you can even vote for the players for the All-Star game.

Baseball Poetry

Casey at the Bat, a Ballad of the Republic, Sung in the Year 1888 by Ernest Lawrence Thayer, is the best-known baseball poem of all time.

Dugout

One letter has been dug out of each of the following common baseball words. Fill in the missing letters. Then, transfer those letters to the corresponding boxes in the grid to form the answer to this riddle: What's another nickname for a baseball bat?

1. U N I _ O R M
2. G _ O V E
3. P L A _ O F F
4. _ L I D E
5. S _ I N G

6. F _ N
7. B U N _
8. C A _ C H E R
9. S T _ A L
10. _ U N

1	2	3	4	5	6	7	8	9	10

UECKER-isms

Bob Uecker was not a particularly good ballplayer. He was a fairly decent catcher but never much of a hitter. He retired from baseball to start a comedy career in which he made fun of himself as a major league ballplayer. Uecker did some very famous commercials, then had his own television show, wrote several books, and even became a baseball broadcaster. He is well known as one of the funniest men ever to play baseball.

Among Uecker's lines …

"Career highlights? I had two. I got an intentional walk from Sandy Koufax and I got out of a rundown against the Mets."

"I knew my career was over. In 1965 my baseball card came out with no picture."

"When I came up to bat with three men on and two outs in the ninth, I looked in the other team's dugout and they were already in street clothes."

"I had no problem catching a knuckleball. I'd just wait until it stopped rolling and pick it up."

Glossary

Assist: When a player makes a throw of any kind to get an out, whether it's an infielder throwing a batter out running to first base or an outfielder throwing a runner out at home plate, the player gets an assist.

Backstop: The fence behind home plate is the backstop. In parks and on little league fields, the backstop is usually a high fence that slants over home plate so that foul balls don't fly off and hurt people passing by.

Bag: Bag is another word for base.

Battery: Battery is a word for the pitcher and catcher. If, for example, Mike Hampton is pitching and Mike Piazza is catching, they are "the battery" in that game.

Batting order: The order in which players on a team come up and take their turn as the hitter. The manager or coach of the team decides the batting order before the game and lists the players, first through ninth, in order of when they will hit. If a batter bats out of turn he is called out.

Bleachers: The seats behind the outfield wall are called the bleachers. Sometimes, like in Wrigley Field, the fans who sit there call themselves the "bleacher bums."

Blooper: A blooper is a ball that is not hit very hard but sort of pops over the infielders and lands in front of the outfielders for a hit.

Box score: A box score is a grid containing a summary of the game statistics, including how each player did.

Bullpen: The bullpen is where the relief pitchers warm up before coming in to pitch. Most stadiums have bullpens beyond the outfield fences, while some have them in foul territory.

Bunt: It's good to learn how to bunt because it can help your team. To bunt is to hold the bat horizontally, one hand on the handle and the other way up on the bat (don't hold it with your hand around the front of the bat, just pinch it from the back part so your finger doesn't get squished by the pitch). The idea is to let the ball just bounce off the bat and stay fair so the runners can move up a base, which is known as a "sacrifice." You can also bunt for a hit by pushing the bat so that the ball rolls a little farther toward third base or first base. Work with a coach to become a good bunter. It helps the team.

Cleanup hitter: The cleanup hitter is the fourth hitter in the lineup.

Closer: The relief pitcher that comes in to get the final outs and the save is the team's "closer."

Commentators: The commentators are the broadcasters or announcers who are at the ballpark describing what is going on in the game on either television or radio.

Commons: Commons are cards that don't have much value because they are only average players. This is the category where most cards fall, but they still may have value to you as a favorite player or a player on your favorite team.

Contact hitter: A contact hitter is one that makes contact with the ball often and doesn't strike out very much.

Count: The count is the number of balls and strikes that have been pitched to the hitter. For example, two balls and two strikes would be a "two and two" count.

Dinger: Dinger is a popular term for a home run!

Disabled list: When a player is injured the team may put the player on what is called "the disabled list," or DL. This means the player cannot play for 15 or more days, and the team can call someone else up from the minor leagues to put on their roster of active players.

Double play: A double play is when two players get called out after one player hits the ball.

Error: When a fielder drops or bobbles a ball or throws it so the other fielder can't catch it and it results in the batter or runner being safe, it's called an error on the fielder.

Extra innings: If a game is tied after the regulation nine innings, teams go into extra innings, which means they play additional innings until someone scores the winning run or runs. The home team always gets the last turn at bat.

Fan: Besides being one of the people rooting for your favorite team, to "fan" in baseball is also another term for striking out.

Foul ball: A ball that is hit that is not in fair territory. Foul balls count as strike one and strike two, but not as strike three unless you're bunting. In the big leagues, most foul balls go into the stands and are souvenirs to the fans who catch them.

Foul line: The lines extending from home plate past first and third base all the way to the outfield fence that separate fair territory from foul territory.

Foul out: When a ball is hit in the air in foul territory and caught by an opposing player for an out.

Foul pole: At every stadium you will see two poles in the outfield at the end of the foul lines. If the ball goes on one side of the pole it's a home run and on the other side it's a foul ball.

Foul territory: The part of the playing field that is outside of the foul lines and not part of the actual field of play.

Full count: Three balls and two strikes is considered a full count—one more ball is a walk and one more strike is a strikeout.

Hit and run: A "hit and run" play is where the runner or runners start running and the batter is supposed to hit the ball on the ground or for a base hit. Actually it should be called "run and hit" since technically the runners start first. This play helps avoid a double play and can also get runners to advance more bases on a base hit.

Hits: A player gets a hit when he or she hits the ball and then runs to the base without making an out. Here are the different kinds of hits you can get:

Single: You get to first base safely without anyone catching the ball in the air, tagging you out, or throwing to first base before you get there.

Double: You get safely to second base.

Triple: You get safely to third base.

Home Run: You touch all the bases including home plate (where you start from as the batter). If you hit one over the fence, it's a home run and you should be very happy!

Grand slam: A grand slam is when you hit a home run with the bases loaded (a player on each base). The most runs you can score on one hit are on a grand slam!

Home team: The team most of the local fans root for since they are the team hosting the game on their field. The home team always bats second in the inning, or in the "bottom of the inning."

Inning: An inning is a period of play in which each team has a turn at bat. Each team gets three outs. A regulation baseball game lasts nine innings.

Inside-the-park home run: Most home runs go over the outfield fence, but a fast runner might be able to get all the way around the bases on a ball that stays in the ballpark on an inside-the-park homer—it's very rare!

Intentional walk: An intentional walk, sometimes called an intentional pass, is when a pitcher walks a batter on purpose. Sometimes this makes it easier to get a double play if there are other runners on second and/or third. Sometimes a batter is walked intentionally because the player is very good and the pitcher doesn't want to give up a home run. It is scored as "IW" or "IBB."

Left on base: You may see this in the box score (LOB) or hear broadcasters mention it. This indicates how many players were left standing on the bases when the final out was made to end an inning.

Mound: The mound, or pitching mound, is the dirt circle in the middle of the infield diamond where the pitcher stands.

On deck: The batter who is scheduled to hit next is considered to be waiting "on deck." Usually there is an on-

deck circle where the player stands and takes practice swings.

Opposite field: When the announcer says a hitter got a hit to the opposite field, it means the ball went the opposite way from where it should go for that type of hitter. When the bat is swung around, most left-handed hitters will hit the ball to right field, and right-handed hitters will hit the ball to left field. If the hitter hits it to the other field, a right-handed hitter hitting to right field and visa versa, it's called hitting to the opposite field.

Over-run: Whoops! This is when you are going too fast and run over the base. Get back fast or you'll be tagged out!

Pennant: The team that wins the National League or American League Championship is said to have won the pennant—then they play in the World Series.

Pickoff: If there's a base runner and the pitcher throws to the fielder, who catches the runner off base and tags that runner for an out, it's called a pickoff. A pickoff at first base would be scored in the corner next to how the runner got on first base: PO 1-3, pickoff, pitcher to first base.

Pinch hitter: A pinch hitter is a hitter who bats in place of someone else.

Pinch runner: A pinch runner is a player who comes in to run for someone else. This may be a faster runner who can steal a base or score a run more easily.

Prospect: A player who is thought to have skills that will make that player a future star is considered to be a prospect.

Putout: Whenever a fielder catches a ball that results in an out, it's a putout. This includes a first baseman taking a throw from an infielder and stepping on the base, or a catcher on a strikeout.

Rain delay: A rain delay is when the game is stopped because of rain, but they hope to continue and finish it later. The umpires decide when to stop, restart, or call a game (call it off) because of rain.

Rain out: A rain out is when a game is called off because of rain. If this happens before the fifth inning, the game doesn't count. If it's after the fifth inning it's considered an official game, and whichever team was ahead at the time wins.

Reliever: A reliever or relief pitcher is the pitcher who comes in to replace the starting pitcher.

Rookie: A first-year player is also known as a rookie.

Roster: A roster is the listing of players on the team. Major league rosters are 25 players for most of the season.

Run: Besides moving your feet faster than walking, a "run" in baseball is whenever a player comes all the way around the bases and crosses home plate. A run scores one point in baseball.

Rundown play: When a runner is trapped between bases, the fielders play what looks like a game of monkey-in-the-middle as they throw the ball back and forth trying to tag the runner and not let him or her get to the next base. Usually a runner will be called out in a rundown play unless one of the fielders misses the ball.

Save: When a pitcher comes into a close ballgame and gets the final outs it is called a save.

Scoring position: When a runner is on second or third base, he is considered in scoring position, meaning it's easier to score on a hit.

Signs: Some people hold up signs in the stands, but in baseball there are other signs. The catcher puts down fingers to give the pitcher a sign as to what pitch to throw. There are also signs relayed from the coach at third base to the batter. Coaches are usually busy touching their cap, tugging on their ear, and doing all sorts of movements. They are signaling the batter to take a pitch, swing away, bunt, or perhaps hit and run. They are also often signaling runners on base. Next time you're at a game, watch the third base coach for a minute and see what he's up to. If you're playing, always check what the sign from the coach is before the pitcher pitches.

Slide: A slide is when a runner dives feet first or head first into a base. Be careful if you try sliding—ask your coach to help you learn how to slide properly so you don't get hurt.

Southpaw: A left-handed pitcher is sometimes referred to as a southpaw.

Spitball or **"spitter":** Once upon a time, in the early years of baseball, it used to be okay for pitchers to spit on the ball before throwing it. It made the ball make some strange movements, and batters had a hard time hitting it. Professional baseball, and most baseball leagues for that matter, have since outlawed the spitball or "spitter."

Starter: The starter is the pitcher that begins pitching the game for the team.

Take: To "take" a pitch means to not swing at it. If a pitcher is having trouble throwing strikes, a batter may take a pitch, or watch one go by, to see if the pitcher can throw it in the strike zone. If the batter has three balls and no strikes, he or she will almost always take the pitch to try and get a "base on balls," or walk to first base.

Tarp: The tarp is what they cover the field with while the teams, umpires, and fans wait for it to stop raining so they can continue the game. It's like a giant piece of plastic that usually just covers the infield.

Triple play: A triple play is a very rare play where one player hits the ball and all three outs are made. Naturally, there has to be no one out and at least two runners on base for a triple play.

Umpire: An umpire is the person who is refereeing the game or ruling on the plays in the game. The umpire rules whether a pitch is a strike or a ball, if a ball that is hit is fair or foul, or if a batter or runner is safe or out. It's a tough job, and many players and fans aren't too crazy about the poor umpires!

Visiting team: The team that comes to play on another team's field. The visiting team always bats first in the inning, known as the "top of the inning," and they often get booed by the home team's fans.

Walk-off home run: A new term, this refers to a home run in the bottom of the ninth or in the home team's at bat in the bottom of an extra inning that wins and ends the game. Following the home run, the teams walk off the field—hence the name.

Wild card: In major league baseball there are three divisions in each league, but four teams make the playoffs each year. The fourth team, the wild card team, is the team in each league with the next best record, or the best second-place team from any one of the three divisions.

Puzzle Answers

page 7 • **Run the Bases**

page 13 • **Curve Ball**

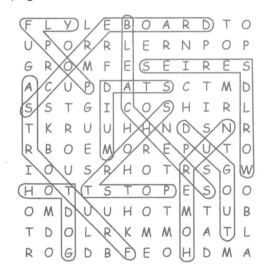

page 14 • **Picture This #1**

Bullpen

page 16 • **Picture This #2**

Southpaw

page 26–27 • **Hard Ball**

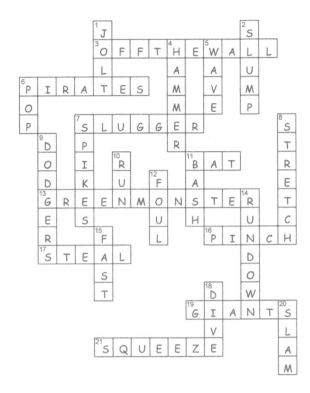

page 42 • **Picture This #3**

Flyball

page 63 • **Play Ball**

1. Print the word "BASEBALL."	BASEBALL
2. Switch the position of the first two letters.	ABSEBALL
3. Move the 5th letter between the 2nd and 3rd letters.	ABBSEALL
4. Switch positions of the 4th and 8th letters.	ABBLEALS
5. Change the 6th letter to a "P."	ABBLEPLS
6. Change the last letter to an "E."	ABBLEPLE
7. Change both "B"s to "P"s.	APPLEPLE
8. Change the 7th letter to an "I."	APPLEPIE

Puzzle Answers

page 65 • Picture This #4

Home run

page 66 • Who's Who?

1. The Big Train
2. Tom Terrific
3. Cyclone
4. Yankee Clipper
5. Double XX
6. Mr. October
7. The Mick
8. Say Hey Kid
9. Stan The Man
10. Charlie Hustle
11. Wizard of Oz
12. The Big Unit
13. The Rocket
14. Big Mac
15. Slammin' Sammy

_3_ Cy Young
_5_ Jimmy Foxx
_4_ Joe DiMaggio
_14_ Mark McGwire
_7_ Mickey Mantle
_11_ Ozzie Smith
_10_ Pete Rose
_12_ Randy Johnson
_6_ Reggie Jackson
_13_ Roger Clemens
_15_ Sammy Sosa
_9_ Stan Musial
_2_ Tom Seaver
_1_ Walter Johnson
_8_ Willie Mays

page 87 • Secret Signals

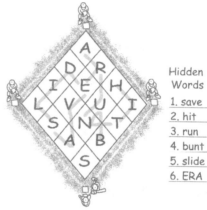

C A R E F U L — T H I S G U Y

I S A P I N C H H I T T E R !

page 88 • Lucky Numbers

9↓	24↓		27↓	13↓
5→ 4	1	12→	5	7
11→ 5	6	15→ 6↓	9	6
17→ 3 15↓	6	8	11↓
16→ 7	9	12→ 4	8
13→ 8	5	1	3

page 102 • Baseball Diamond

Hidden Words
1. save
2. hit
3. run
4. bunt
5. slide
6. ERA

page 78 • Seventh Inning Stretch

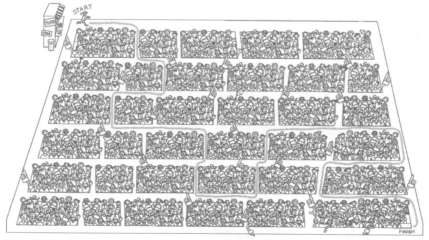

133

Puzzle Answers

page 109 • Score!

Players	1	2	3	4	5	6	7	8	9	10	11	AB	R	H	RBI
Rose (5)	◇	◇	◇	K	◇	◇		◇	E3		◇	◇	◇		S
Morgan (4)	HR		◇	◇	S	◇	E3	◇		◇	◇	◇			◇
Bench (2)	◇	◇	E3	◇	K	E3	◇		K	◇	E3		◇		◇
Perez (3)	◇	◇	K		◇	◇	HR		◇	K	◇	◇	◇		◇
Foster (7)		E3	◇	◇	◇		S		◇	E3	◇				
Griffey (9)	◇	K	◇		◇	◇	◇	◇	◇			K	◇	K	
Geronimo (8)	◇	S	◇	K	◇	◇	◇		◇			HR			
Gullet (1)	K	E3		◇	◇		◇	K	◇	◇	K				
Carroll (6)	◇		◇	K	E3	◇	◇	◇		◇		E3			◇
McEnaney (10)	◇	K	◇	◇	◇		E3		◇	K	◇	K	◇	◇	

page 110 • Say What?

Y	O		H		I		N	O	M			O		R	E			
T	O	G	I	I	T		C	A	T	E	T	H	E	R	E	A	D	
Y	O	G	I		,	I		C	A	M	E		H	E	R	E		
T	O		H	I	T		,	N	O	T		T	O		R	E	A	D	!

page 112 • The Magic Number

The season has 162 scheduled games.		
	won	lost
TEAM A	93	59
TEAM B	89	63

games TEAM B has won	89
ADD games TEAM B has left	+10
	= 99
SUBTRACT games TEAM A has won	−93
	= 6
ADD the number 1	+1
THE MAGIC NUMBER	= 7

page 117 • Collectible Card

HANK AARON

RIGHTFEILDER

ATLANTA BRAVES

page 124 • Extra In-nings

1. BEG IN = to start
   (to plead for money)

2. CAB IN = a small house in the woods
   (taxi)

3. ROB IN = a springtime bird with a red breast
   (steal)

4. SAT IN = a heavy, shiny fabric
   (past tense of sit)

5. PUFF IN = penguin-like bird with a colorful beak
   (short breath out)

page 127 • Dugout

1	2	3	4	5	6	7	8	9	10
F	L	Y	S	W	A	T	T	E	R

Index

We Have EVERYTHING!

OVER TWO MILLION EVERYTHING. BOOKS SOLD

Everything® **After College Book**
$12.95, 1-55850-847-3

Everything® **Angels Book**
$12.95, 1-58062-398-0

Everything® **Astrology Book**
$12.95, 1-58062-062-0

Everything® **Baby Names Book**
$12.95, 1-55850-655-1

Everything® **Baby Shower Book**
$12.95, 1-58062-305-0

Everything® **Baby's First Food Book**
$12.95, 1-58062-512-6

Everything® **Barbeque Cookbook**
$12.95, 1-58062-316-6

Everything® **Bartender's Book**
$9.95, 1-55850-536-9

Everything® **Bedtime Story Book**
$12.95, 1-58062-147-3

Everything® **Bicycle Book**
$12.00, 1-55850-706-X

Everything® **Build Your Own Home Page**
$12.95, 1-58062-339-5

Everything® **Business Planning Book**
$12.95, 1-58062-491-X

Everything® **Casino Gambling Book**
$12.95, 1-55850-762-0

Everything® **Cat Book**
$12.95, 1-55850-710-8

Everything® **Chocolate Cookbook**
$12.95, 1-58062-405-7

Everything® **Christmas Book**
$15.00, 1-55850-697-7

Everything® **Civil War Book**
$12.95, 1-58062-366-2

Everything® **College Survival Book**
$12.95, 1-55850-720-5

Everything® **Computer Book**
$12.95, 1-58062-401-4

Everything® **Cookbook**
$14.95, 1-58062-400-6

Everything® **Cover Letter Book**
$12.95, 1-58062-312-3

Everything® **Crossword and Puzzle Book**
$12.95, 1-55850-764-7

Everything® **Dating Book**
$12.95, 1-58062-185-6

Everything® **Dessert Book**
$12.95, 1-55850-717-5

Everything® **Dog Book**
$12.95, 1-58062-144-9

Everything® **Dreams Book**
$12.95, 1-55850-806-6

Everything® **Etiquette Book**
$12.95, 1-55850-807-4

Everything® **Family Tree Book**
$12.95, 1-55850-763-9

Everything® **Fly-Fishing Book**
$12.95, 1-58062-148-1

Everything® **Games Book**
$12.95, 1-55850-643-8

Everything® **Get-A-Job Book**
$12.95, 1-58062-223-2

Everything® **Get Published Book**
$12.95, 1-58062-315-8

Everything® **Get Ready for Baby Book**
$12.95, 1-55850-844-9

Everything® **Golf Book**
$12.95, 1-55850-814-7

Everything® **Guide to Las Vegas**
$12.95, 1-58062-438-3

Everything® **Guide to New York City**
$12.95, 1-58062-314-X

Everything® **Guide to Walt Disney World®, Universal Studios®, and Greater Orlando, 2nd Edition**
$12.95, 1-58062-404-9

Everything® **Guide to Washington D.C.**
$12.95, 1-58062-313-1

Everything® **Herbal Remedies Book**
$12.95, 1-58062-331-X

Everything® **Home-Based Business Book**
$12.95, 1-58062-364-6

Everything® **Homebuying Book**
$12.95, 1-58062-074-4

Everything® **Homeselling Book**
$12.95, 1-58062-304-2

Everything® **Home Improvement Book**
$12.95, 1-55850-718-3

Everything® **Hot Careers Book**
$12.95, 1-58062-486-3

Everything® **Internet Book**
$12.95, 1-58062-073-6

Everything® **Investing Book**
$12.95, 1-58062-149-X

Everything® **Jewish Wedding Book**
$12.95, 1-55850-801-5

Everything® **Job Interviews Book**
$12.95, 1-58062-493-6

Everything® **Lawn Care Book**
$12.95, 1-58062-487-1

Everything® **Leadership Book**
$12.95, 1-58062-513-4

Everything® **Low-Fat High-Flavor Cookbook**
$12.95, 1-55850-802-3

Everything® **Magic Book**
$12.95, 1-58062-418-9

Everything® **Microsoft® Word 2000 Book**
$12.95, 1-58062-306-9

For more information, or to order, call 800-872-5627
or visit everything.com

Adams Media Corporation, 260 Center Street, Holbrook, MA 02343

Available wherever books are sold!

Everything® **Money Book**
$12.95, 1-58062-145-7

Everything® **Mother Goose Book**
$12.95, 1-58062-490-1

Everything® **Mutual Funds Book**
$12.95, 1-58062-419-7

Everything® **One-Pot Cookbook**
$12.95, 1-58062-186-4

Everything® **Online Business Book**
$12.95, 1-58062-320-4

Everything® **Online Genealogy Book**
$12.95, 1-58062-402-2

Everything® **Online Investing Book**
$12.95, 1-58062-338-7

Everything® **Online Job Search Book**
$12.95, 1-58062-365-4

Everything® **Pasta Book**
$12.95, 1-55850-719-1

Everything® **Pregnancy Book**
$12.95, 1-58062-146-5

Everything® **Pregnancy Organizer**
$15.00, 1-58062-336-0

Everything® **Quick Meals Cookbook**
$12.95, 1-58062-488-X

Everything® **Resume Book**
$12.95, 1-58062-311-5

Everything® **Sailing Book**
$12.95, 1-58062-187-2

Everything® **Selling Book**
$12.95, 1-58062-319-0

Everything® **Study Book**
$12.95, 1-55850-615-2

Everything® **Tall Tales, Legends, and Outrageous Lies Book**
$12.95, 1-58062-514-2

Everything® **Tarot Book**
$12.95, 1-58062-191-0

Everything® **Time Management Book**
$12.95, 1-58062-492-8

Everything® **Toasts Book**
$12.95, 1-58062-189-9

Everything® **Total Fitness Book**
$12.95, 1-58062-318-2

Everything® **Trivia Book**
$12.95, 1-58062-143-0

Everything® **Tropical Fish Book**
$12.95, 1-58062-343-3

Everything® **Vitamins, Minerals, and Nutritional Supplements Book**
$12.95, 1-58062-496-0

Everything® **Wedding Book, 2nd Edition**
$12.95, 1-58062-190-2

Everything® **Wedding Checklist**
$7.95, 1-58062-456-1

Everything® **Wedding Etiquette Book**
$7.95, 1-58062-454-5

Everything® **Wedding Organizer**
$15.00, 1-55850-828-7

Everything® **Wedding Shower Book**
$7.95, 1-58062-188-0

Everything® **Wedding Vows Book**
$7.95, 1-58062-455-3

Everything® **Wine Book**
$12.95, 1-55850-808-2

Everything® **Angels Mini Book**
$4.95, 1-58062-387-5

Everything® **Astrology Mini Book**
$4.95, 1-58062-385-9

Everything® **Baby Names Mini Book**
$4.95, 1-58062-391-3

Everything® **Bedtime Story Mini Book**
$4.95, 1-58062-390-5

Everything® **Dreams Mini Book**
$4.95, 1-58062-386-7

Everything® **Etiquette Mini Book**
$4.95, 1-58062-499-5

Everything® **Get Ready for Baby Mini Book**
$4.95, 1-58062-389-1

Everything® **Golf Mini Book**
$4.95, 1-58062-500-2

Everything® **Love Spells Mini Book**
$4.95, 1-58062-388-3

Everything® **Pregnancy Mini Book**
$4.95, 1-58062-392-1

Everything® **TV & Movie Trivia Mini Book**
$4.95, 1-58062-497-9

Everything® **Wine Mini Book**
$4.95, 1-58062-498-7

Everything® **Kids' Baseball Book**
$9.95, 1-58062-489-8

Everything® **Kids' Joke Book**
$9.95, 1-58062-495-2

Everything® **Kids' Money Book**
$9.95, 1-58062-322-0

Everything® **Kids' Nature Book**
$9.95, 1-58062-321-2

Everything® **Kids' Online Book**
$9.95, 1-58062-394-8

Everything® **Kids' Puzzle Book**
$9.95, 1-58062-323-9

Everything® **Kids' Space Book**
$9.95, 1-58062-395-6

Everything® **Kids' Witches and Wizards Book**
$9.95, 1-58062-396-4

Everything® is a registered trademark of Adams Media Corporation.

For more information, or to order, call 800-872-5627 or visit everything.com
Adams Media Corporation, 260 Center Street, Holbrook, MA 02343

We Have
EVERYTHING KIDS'!

Everything® Kids' Baseball Book
$9.95, 1-58062-489-8

Everything® Kids' Joke Book
$9.95, 1-58062-495-2

Everything® Kids' Money Book
$9.95, 1-58062-322-0

Everything® Kids' Nature Book
$9.95, 1-58062-321-2

Everything® Kids' Online Book
$9.95, 1-58062-394-8

Everything® Kids' Puzzle Book
$9.95, 1-58062-323-9

Everything® Kids' Space Book
$9.95, 1-58062-395-6

Everything® Kids' Witches and Wizards
$9.95, 1-58062-39

Available wherever books are sold!

For more information, or to order,
call 800-872-5627 or visit everything.com

Adams Media Corporation, 260 Center Street, Holbrook, MA 02343

Everything® is a registered trademark of Adams Media Corporation